How Scotland is Owned

SCOTLAND

This book is based on an in-depth study by the author, sponsored by WWF Scotland – part of the World Wide Fund for Nature – an organisation dedicated to the improvement of humanity's relationships with nature. Most of WWF's work is aimed at promoting improvements which can be achieved through central government policy and legislation. Land tenure is of particular interest to WWF because of the link, highlighted in this book, between a nation's system of land tenure and the sustainable management, or *stewardship*, of its natural resources. We believe that stewardship, embodying the principle of legitimate use for human benefit – but with a duty of responsibility to future generations and to the wider community – is a concept of increasing relevance and value in Scotland as elsewhere in the world. The author's study on land tenure forms part of an ongoing programme of work sponsored by WWF Scotland on this theme.

Simon Pepper
Head of WWF Scotland
8 The Square
Aberfeldy PH15 2DD
Telephone: 01887 820449

How Scotland is Owned

Robin Callander

CANONGATE

First published in Great Britain in 1998 by
Canongate Books Ltd.,
14 High Street, Edinburgh EH1 1TE

10 9 8 7 6 5 4 3 2 1

British Library Cataloguing-in-Publication Data
A catalogue record for this book is available on request
from the British Library

ISBN 0 86241 772 4

Typeset by Palimpsest Book Production Limited
Polmont, Stirlingshire

Printed and bound by Biddles, Guildford

Contents

Foreword

by Andy Wightman

How Scotland is Owned is a work of tremendous legal and political significance. Not only does it stand alone in subjecting Scotland's system of land tenure to a remarkably thorough and powerful review and critique, it does so at a very appropriate time. Whilst there is a general awareness of the pattern, politics and social impacts of landownership, most people remain blissfully unaware of what land tenure is, what it is designed to do, what the current system consists of and how it evolved. This book fills that gap and represents a crucial contribution to the growing debate about land reform.

Land tenure governs the fundamental relationship between the people of Scotland and the territory which they occupy. As this book makes clear, land tenure covers not only the rights of owners and occupiers of land, but includes matters as diverse as royal animals, the ownership of the marine environment, the role of the Crown, public access, the status of freshwater mussels and the common interests of tenement dwellers.

Land tenure governs the way in which society defines and distributes rights in land. It is the mechanism by which power over property is derived, held, distributed and exercised and it is the means by which a balance is reached between legitimate private interests on the one hand and public interests on the other. This book provides the first comprehensive analysis of this system and of how it might be modernised and updated.

Those who are familiar with Robin Callander's writing will be aware of the rigour and depth of his research. I first became aware of this when I read his 1987 book *A Pattern of Landownership in Scotland*. It is the kind of book which reveals new insights into the subject at each new reading and it is a book which remains the only comprehensive and authoritative review of Scotland's landowning history to be published in the 20th century. Unfortunately it also remains out of print.

Robin Callander may not be widely known but he is without doubt the foremost thinker on land tenure in Scotland. He was the instigator of the successful John McEwen Memorial Lectures on land tenure and has produced an impressive body of writing on the subject. Callander is not a lawyer or academic and his work is rooted in his practical involvement in rural land use and community development. He has explored the complexities of Scottish land law and frequently uncovered areas which have been perhaps conveniently ignored or forgotten about. In doing so he has earned the respect of academics and lawyers.

It is significant in this regard that this book has been produced by someone from outwith the legal and landed establishment, a body of opinion which has on many occasions promoted the view that land tenure is a purely technical subject which is best left to them to consider. This book is an eloquent reminder that the practitioners of a subject are not always in the best position to advise the rest of us on matters of such fundamental public interest as to how we define and distribute the rights of property.

In Callander's analysis of Scotland's land tenure system he develops a compelling argument for reform in order to strengthen and modernise this important area of civil law. In this context it is worth stressing that the attention given to the role of the Crown in Callander's argument is not some mere theoretical or academic point. It is fundamental to retaining and developing a legal framework which provides a mechanism for balancing public and private interests, rights and obligations. It is a point which the political and legal establishment needs to take on board urgently if land tenure reform is to do anything other than satisfy shallow political or legal ambitions.

Furthermore the role of the Crown emphasises perhaps the most crucial aspect of Scotland's land laws, namely that not only do these laws belong to the people as a whole to amend as they see fit but that perfect authority legally and morally exists for them to do so. Given the current proposals to abolish feudal superiorities, for example, it is instructive to be reminded that whilst feudal tenure has its faults it also has the immense advantage (not shared by many other tenure systems) that it is still a conditional system where those who hold land do so on terms which derive from society as a whole through the Crown.

How Scotland is Owned does not pretend to be an easy book to read or understand at a first reading. It deals with some demanding constitutional and legal issues. But a system of land tenure which has evolved under the control of its main beneficiaries for the best part of 1000 years is not going to be reformed without us first making the effort to understand it. Whatever one's interest in the topic this book makes for a challenging and stimulating read and will repay the effort of those who make it.

Preface and Acknowledgements

This book examines Scotland's unique system of land tenure as a contribution to the rapidly developing debate about how the long-standing issue of land reform in Scotland might be tackled by the new Scottish Parliament.

The pattern of land ownership has already been well described in books on 'Who Owns Scotland' by John McEwen in 1977 and Andy Wightman in 1996. Now, as the prospect of land reform increases, so does the need for a wider understanding of the actual system of land ownership. It is that system, Scotland's system of land tenure, that provides the legal framework governing all aspects of how Scotland is owned.

The purpose of this book is to encourage greater discussion about that system by providing a wide ranging description of it. The book is based on a review of Scotland's system of land tenure that I wrote in 1996-97. I am very grateful to WWF Scotland for funding that work and for their permission to use parts of the review in this book. However, it should be clearly recognised that I, and not WWF Scotland, am responsible for the views and opinions I express in this book.

Readers should also be warned that the book is not a light and easy read! Scotland's system of land tenure is notoriously arcane and complex at the best of times and this book deals with it at a fairly technical level. For too long knowledge of the system has been largely the preserve of specialist lawyers. This need not and should not be the case and hopefully this book can help more people to have a broad grasp of the full scope and nature of the system.

The book covers many different aspects of Scots law and I readily acknowledge that I have no formal legal qualifications. My own professional involvements are in rural development and land use issues and this book should be seen against that background. It is a

response to the lack of an equivalent book by someone better qualified and I am very grateful to all the people who have contributed
to my own understanding of Scotland's system of land tenure. In
particular, I am pleased to have this opportunity to thank Simon
Pepper of WWF Scotland for all his invaluable support and advice
during my work with WWF Scotland on land tenure. I am also
indebted to the following for helpful discussions, advice and
comments during that work:

Gerald Barry, Graham Boyd, Professor John Bryden, Derek Flyn,
Dermot Grimson, Alan Hampson, Dr James Hunter, Sir Malcolm
Innes, Elizabeth Leighton, Professor Greg Lloyd, Professor David
McCrone, Professor Bryan MacGregor, Professor Neil MacCormick,
John Randall, Andrew Raven, Nick Reiter, Professor Colin Reid,
Professor Ken Reid, Sheila Ritchie, David Rothe, Professor Jeremy
Rowan Robinson, Duncan Thomson, John Watt and Andy
Wightman.

I would especially like to thank Andy Wightman for all our
discussions and joint ventures on the issue of land ownership in
Scotland and to acknowledge all the help I have had with the book
from Donald Reid and Hugh Andrew of Canongate Books. The
responsibility for any mistakes of fact, interpretation, representation
or emphasis is, of course, mine.

Finally, I dedicate the book to Rita, Ailidh, Isla and Corrie for all
their support, sympathy and tolerance while I was writing it.

Robin Callander
Finzean, February 1998

Introduction

The debate about land ownership in Scotland has recently entered a crucial new phase. While there have long been calls in Scotland for land reform, the likelihood of it actually occurring improved dramatically over the space of a few months in 1997 with the election of a government with a manifesto commitment to land reform and then the even more emphatic vote for the Scottish Parliament. These developments have shifted the focus of the debate from why to what, from making the case for change to the less familiar issue of the nature of the changes required. Central to tackling this issue is understanding Scotland's system of land tenure.

The term *tenure* derives from the Latin (and French) word for *to hold* and every sovereign country, Scotland included, has a system of land tenure to govern who has what rights over which parts of that country's land. Scotland's system, like the equivalent systems in other countries, spans all aspects of *How Scotland is Owned*, from the sovereign rights by which the territory of Scotland is held, down to the legal rights and responsibilities that are held by the owners and occupiers of lands and buildings in Scotland. Most people in Scotland are therefore directly involved in the system, as a tenant or owner of their home, while more generally the system has a pervasive influence over the whole country.

Scotland's system of land tenure is different from that in the rest of Britain because it is determined by Scots law and also unique in the modern world because it is still legally classified as a feudal system. Feudal tenure first became established in Scotland during the 11th century and remarkably, while it has undergone many important changes since then, it has survived for nearly 1000 years as the main basis of land ownership in Scotland. The simple fact that Scotland's system of land tenure is still feudal is indicative of the need for change and the aim of this book is both to describe that system and to suggest ways it might be modernised and reformed. The Scottish Parliament could replace this ancient system with one that is more supportive of Scotland's contemporary requirements for economic development, social justice and environmental stewardship.

A major problem in that task is that Scotland's existing system of land tenure is a particularly extensive, archaic and complex area of Scots law. While this reflects the system's broad scope, long history and detailed legal nature, it has encouraged the view that knowledge of land tenure is something that is only accessible to trained lawyers. In particular, this has created a gap between, on the one hand, all those both inside and outside government who are involved with economic, social and environmental policy issues and yet tend to have little understanding of the current system of land tenure, and on the other hand, lawyers and related specialist groups who are familiar with the intricacies of Scots land law, but who usually have a limited knowledge of the wider policy issues. A key aim of this book is to help bridge that gap by providing a 'map' that clarifies the structure and character of Scotland's distinctive system of land tenure and its main component parts. The absence of such a framework has continued to be an obstacle to constructive discussions about land tenure reform.

A central theme of the book is the role of the land tenure system in determining the balance of public and private interests in Scotland's land. An important starting point is to recognise that the 'public interest' is involved at three levels. At one level, the public interest is represented by Parliament and the democratic authority that Parliament has *over* the whole system of land tenure. Below this, however, the public interest is also represented at two levels by legal rights held by the public *within* the system. The most fundamental of these are the sovereign rights by which the whole territory of Scotland is held – the land and surrounding territorial seas, together with all the natural resources associated with these areas above and below the ground. These rights, which are held 'in trust' for the public through the Crown, are the basis of the land tenure system and the rights of ownership held by land owners derive from them. The third and final level at which the public interest is represented is where land is owned by a public body (such as the Forestry Commission) rather than a private land owner.

The main focus in this book is on the second of these levels – the public rights held in all Scotland's land through the Crown. These rights represent the public interest within the framework that the system of land tenure provides for both public and private rights in the ownership and management of land in Scotland. It is Parliament which then adjusts and adapts this framework to ensure an appropriate balance is maintained.

This balance between public and private interests is explained more fully in the first two sections of the book. The first section describes the historical background to Scotland's current system of land tenure, the momentum that has built up in rural and urban Scotland for the reform of the system, the reasons why land tenure reform is an issue likely to be tackled early in the life of the Scottish Parliament and the main aims that might be adopted to guide any reforms. The second section then outlines the main constitutional and legal ingredients of Scotland's system of land tenure, starting with the position of the Crown in the system. The rights vested in the Crown are set in the context of the authority of Parliament and what is meant by 'land ownership'. The next two sections then provide a systematic description of the areas of Scotland's territory held by the Crown in the public interest, the rights retained by the Crown in the rest of Scotland's land and the rights that are held by owners over those areas.

The book is therefore not about the wider aspects of land reform and does not consider, for example, the contentious issue of the redistribution of land in Scotland. Also, while the book concentrates on the system of land tenure, it does not aim to be a critique that starts with the worst excesses of the current system and then works on down through its many adverse consequences. The structure of the contents reflects that the approach of the book is to review the current system by describing its main components in order and commenting on the way through on some of the elements of the system that might be most usefully retained or replaced. These suggestions are then pulled together in the final chapters to illustrate the types of land tenure reforms that the Scottish Parliament might consider.

The purpose of the book is to provide a framework for discussions about the potential for a thorough modernisation and reform of Scotland's overall system of land tenure to meet Scotland's needs in a new millennium after all but 1000 years of feudalism. The book covers many aspects of law from the nuances of constitutional law to the details of leasing land and is ambitious in its scope. However, a wide ranging and exploratory review of the type in this book is an important part of both bridging the gap between policy makers and legal experts and encouraging a constructive debate more generally in Scotland about land tenure reform. That debate is required, as Andy Wightman and others have warned, if the system of land ownership in Scotland is going to be successfully reformed at the start of the new millennium in ways that promote the sustainable management of Scotland's land and natural resources for both current and future generations.

SECTION ONE
The Current System of Land Ownership

CHAPTER ONE

Scotland's Feudal System

The Pattern of Estates

The pattern of land ownership in a country is a telling measure of its system of land tenure and it is no coincidence that Scotland is both the only country in the world with a feudal system of land tenure and the country with the most concentrated pattern of large-scale private estates.

The results of Andy Wightman's researches for his 1996 book *Who Owns Scotland* confirmed that less than 1500 private owners still own the majority of Scotland's land area. Amongst these largest private estates, the pattern is dominated by fewer and larger estates: 50% of Scotland's 19 million acres is held by 608 land owners, 40% by 283, 30% by 136, 20% by 58 and 10% by 18.[1]

These statistics, remarkable as they are for a modern western democracy with a population of five million, actually underplay the extent to which the private ownership of Scotland's countryside is concentrated into very few hands. The statistics above are calculated using the total land area of Scotland, 12% of which is owned by public bodies (such as the Forestry Commission) and another 3% of which is covered by Scotland's main cities and towns. Taking this 15% out of the equation means that over half of the privately owned land in rural Scotland is held by less than 350 owners, each with estates of over 7500 acres, and over a third by less than 125 owners with 20,000 acres or more each. For comparison, even 100 years ago when England was still considered to be dominated by large estates, less than 7% of England's land was held in estates of 20,000 acres or more. It appears no other country in the world can match the concentrated private ownership in Scotland. Places that might have provided similar patterns, for example most of the countries in South America, have all had programmes of land reform during the last 50 years. Those reforms resulted from the influence of the United Nations which, since the 1950s, has recognised concentrated patterns of land ownership as an obstacle to economic development and required land reform as a condition of development aid.

Another remarkable feature of the pattern of land ownership in Scotland is the degree of continuity it has shown since feudal tenure was introduced in Scotland in the 11th century. Ever since, the majority of Scotland's land has always been held by less than 1500 owners.[2] Estimates suggest that by the 13th century, when the Crown and Church owned many large estates, there were only about 2000 land owners in total in Scotland. This number continued to increase until the 17th century, by when virtually all the former Crown and Church lands were in private ownership and there were approximately 10,000 land owners in Scotland. However, only 1500 of these were major land owners.

In the 17th century, the trend of the earlier centuries reversed and the overall number of land owners started to decline. This continued throughout the 18th century and into the early 19th century, by which time the number of land owners in Scotland was down to around 7500. The fall was due to a reduction in the number of small land owners and the extent of Scotland held by the 1500 largest estates showed a marked increase. These estates maintained their position during the 19th century, and in the 1870s, when there was the only ever government survey of land ownership, it found that over 90% of Scotland's land was still held by less than 1500 owners.

During the 20th century, the proportion of Scotland owned by the 1500 largest private estates has fallen from over 90% to around 60%. This reduction is very largely accounted for by the growth in the amount of land owned by the state, the increase of owner-occupied farms in parts of Scotland and the spread of urbanisation. Within the 60%, with the exception of reductions in size of some of the very largest estates (for example, the Duke of Sutherland's vast 19th century estate of over one million acres), the overall estate structure has remained fairly constant. The number of estates in Scotland with over 1000 acres, for example, only reduced from 1758 to 1723 between the 1870s and 1970s. In some districts of Scotland, if house owners with five acres or less were excluded, the number of land owners in the 1970s had not yet returned to the level of the mid 17th century, before the major and often overlooked re-concentration of land ownership in Scotland in the 200 years 1650–1850.[3]

Historical analysis of the overall extent and pattern of large estates in Scotland shows that they owe more to events and trends over previous centuries than to recent influences. Similarly, a high pro-portion of these estates is still owned by families that have been major land owners in Scotland for many centuries.[4] These factors suggest that there is still a certain resonance to the statement by the early 19th century authority on land ownership and management in Scotland, Sir John Sinclair, who said: "In no other country in Europe are the rights of proprietors so well defined and so well protected".[5]

Feudal Tenure

The ownership of land in Scotland has always granted wide-ranging rights over that land and these rights have conferred economic, social and political advantages on their holders.[6] However, within Scotland's system of feudal tenure, the distribution of these rights between land owners does not coincide with the pattern of land holdings on a map. The owners of land do not own their land outright and their authority over that land has always been constrained not only by the general laws of the country, but also by the nature of their feudal title to their land.

Feudal land ownership in Scotland is a hierarchical system within which all the rights of land ownership derive from the highest authority in Scotland. In legal theory, this is God, but in practice it is the Crown who is taken as the ultimate owner of all of Scotland. The Crown is known as the Paramount Superior and all other land owners are known as vassals of the Crown.

The essential feature of Scotland's feudal tenure is that the relationship between the Crown and its vassals need not be direct. Within the system, not only are certain rights reserved by the Crown but anyone, when they dispose of land they own in Scotland, can retain an interest in that land through the terms of the title deed conveying the land to the new owner. They, as a vassal of the Crown, then become the superior of the new owner, who becomes their vassal. There is no limit in Scots law to the number of times this process, known as subinfeudation or feuing, can be repeated over the same piece of ground. At each stage, superiors can limit the extent of possession conveyed by reserving rights to themselves (for example, mineral rights) and by imposing additional burdens and conditions on the vassals (for example, that the new owner has to obtain the superior's permission to erect any new building or carry on any trade or business on the land). While feuing land creates new superior-vassal relationships, land can be sold outright so that the new owner replaces the former as a vassal.

This system creates a hierarchy of interests in any piece of land and maintains a traditional feudal pyramid over the land of Scotland that runs down from God and the Paramount Superior at its apex, through superiors, to the vassals at its base in actual possession of the land. These chains of superior-vassal relationships or tenure, and the different reservations and burdens at each stage, mean that the distribution of property rights in Scotland is dramatically more complex than the pattern of land holdings. However, this feudal system can be viewed as forming basically three levels of ownership.

The highest level is the interests of the Crown, known in legal terms as the *regalia*. These principally consist of the sovereign rights that are held inalienably by the Crown (for example, over the sea within territorial waters) and other property rights which are reserved to the Crown but which, in contrast to inalienable rights, can be granted out to other owners (for example, salmon fishings). The second level is the interests of superiority or, in legal terms, the *dominium directum* (direct ownership). A right of pre-emption is, in addition to the examples given above, one of the rights commonly retained by superiors. This is a right of first offer to buy back a property if a vassal should decide to sell.

The third level of ownership is the interests of the vassal in possession of the land or, in legal terms, the *dominium utile* (useful ownership). Their rights are subject to all the reservations and burdens of their feudal superiors. Below this level are tenants, who derive their rights of occupation and use from the vassal. The position of tenants is as old as the feudal system and although the status of tenants is traditionally contrasted with that of owners, the legislation governing tenancies has always made tenants fully integrated components of Scotland's system of land tenure.

This feudal hierarchy of interests dates from the introduction of feudalism in Scotland. The Crown assumed ownership of all the land in the realm and then granted out authority over different parts of the land to others in exchange for financial and military obligations to the Crown. These owners could then grant out portions of their lands to others under similar conditions to enable them to meet their commitments to the Crown. This process then continued on down through several levels of superiors and vassals. Originally vassals mainly held their land under what was termed 'wardhold'. This obliged them, amongst other conditions, to support their superiors with men at arms as often as was called for. Wardholds were abolished in 1746, following the Jacobite Rebellion that ended at Culloden. They were all converted into 'feuholds' which, again amongst other conditions, obliged vassals to pay an annual fee or feu duty to their superior. Feuholds or feuing is still the method by which almost all land is owned in Scotland and the character of this relationship has changed remarkably little since the mid 18th century. A key change was that, in 1974, the imposition of new feu duties was prohibited and feu holders were given the right to redeem (buy out) existing feu duties. In earlier times, feu duties had been set as economic rents but most had become more or less nominal payments by the 1970s.

Not all land in Scotland is held under feudal tenure. There is land held under what is called alloidal tenure, in which the land is held subject to no superior. Examples of this type of land include some Crown and Church of Scotland lands, land acquired by compulsory purchase and land in the Northern Isles still held under the ancient system of udal tenure. These exceptions are examined later. The point here is that nearly all privately owned land in Scotland is held under feudal tenure and the survival of such characteristically feudal elements as superiorities and feu duties is indicative of the extraordinarily archaic and complex nature of Scotland's current system of land ownership.

Law Reform Committees

For over 30 years, successive governments and a broad consensus of legal opinion in Scotland have been of the view that Scotland's system of feudal tenure should be replaced.

In the 1960s, the Secretaries of State for Scotland appointed a series of committees of legal experts to report on aspects of reforming land tenure in Scotland.[7] The reports of these committees were followed in 1969 by a government green paper *Land Tenure in Scotland – A Plan for Reform*, and in 1972 by a white paper *Land Tenure Reform in Scotland*. As a result, some initial legislation was enacted during the 1970s with the Conveyancing and Feudal Reform (Scotland) Act 1970, the Land Tenure Reform (Scotland) Act 1974 and the Land Registration (Scotland) Act 1979. These acts brought about a range of changes, which included limiting the rights of pre-emption held by superiors from a perpetual right to a once-only option (1970), prohibiting the creation of new feu duties and enabling existing feu duties to be redeemed (1974) and setting up a systematic register to record the ownership of land in Scotland (1979).

Many of the changes in the 1970s legislation were both of significant practical value and of a historic nature, given the long-standing character of some of the issues tackled. However, they did not end feudal tenure and in the 1980s, the Scottish Law Commission (SLC), the government's official law reform agency, started work on proposals to complete this task.[8] After several years work, in 1991 the SLC published a 200 page discussion paper entitled *Abolition of the Feudal System*. After public consultation on their proposals, the SLC undertook to produce a further report. That was then rescheduled several times over the following years until 1997, when the SLC set out a new programme of work up until 1999 to tackle the topic.[9]

The SLC's 1991 report contained proposals on a range of tenurial issues, but the two main topics were the final removal of feu duties after the partial reforms of the 1974 Act and the abolition of feudal superiorities. It is surprising that the SLC did not then or subsequently draft the relatively straightforward legislation required to finally remove all feu duties. The SLC themselves argued that this uncontroversial measure would bring a number of social and economic benefits and simplify later changes to the land tenure system. The abolition of feu duties could also have been linked to removing the other surviving duties and charges still associated with the feudal system (for example, teinds and stipends which were originally charges to support local ministers). However, in the context here, feu duties are an example that does illustrate that some elements of the feudal system can be dealt with fairly separately.

In contrast, the other main topic in the SLC's 1991 report, superiorities, demonstrates the limited scope for abolishing some other parts of the feudal system before wider questions have been tackled. The abolition of feudal superiorities, unlike the simple removal of feu duties, requires clarification of what new arrangements are to replace them. There are two main aspects to this. Firstly, the implications for the Crown, which will no longer be the Paramount Superior, in name at least. Secondly, whether there are to be alternative arrangements for the types of rights and interests currently governed by feudal superiorities.

The removal of the Crown's title of Paramount Superior would not alter the fact that the Crown would retain ultimate ownership of the whole realm. However, what would be the former Paramount Superior's status, role and rights in the reformed system? The SLC's proposals did not consider these issues fully. They did not, for example, seek to clarify the *regalia* or rights held by the Crown, despite the fact that the extent and nature of these is not even clear in the current system.[10] The abolition of feudal superiorities would create a direct relationship between the Crown and all land owners. Clarification of the Crown's rights and interests has an important bearing on the nature of that relationship and is examined later in this book (Section 3).

The second broad question identified above is the nature of the relationships between different owners following the abolition of feudal superiorities. The SLC's proposals involved establishing a system of *land conditions* that would, rather surprisingly, largely reinstate many key features of the superiority system that was being abolished. The question of retaining such a system of private regulation by one owner over other owners, however, raises wider issues than were addressed by the SLC and which are considered in more detail later in this book (Section 4).

These points illustrate that there is limited scope to modernise land tenure in Scotland simply by abolishing parts of the existing feudal system. Where elements of the system need to be replaced, fuller consideration has to be given to the aims and nature of the new system that is to be put in place. This is then likely, as elaborated below, to lead to the identification of further elements of the current system where modernisation is required. A much fuller review is thus a necessary part of the modernisation process.

Narrow Legal Focus

In their 1991 report, the SLC claimed that their proposals would amount to the introduction of a 'new system' of land tenure in Scotland. The SLC restated this position in 1997:

> Almost all land in Scotland continues to be held on feudal tenure . . .
> Our aim is to abolish this system . . . and replace it with a modern
> system . . . The case for abolition is well documented and not
> seriously disputed.[11]

The SLC are correct to suggest that there is a broad consensus for abolishing feudal tenure. The uncontroversial nature of this is illustrated by the support of the government and bodies like the Scottish Landowners Federation.[12] However, the SLC's apparently momentous claim to be introducing a new system of land tenure in Scotland needs to be viewed with considerable caution. The scope of Scotland's system of land tenure goes much wider than simply its feudal elements and replacing feudal tenure would only amount to introducing a new form of tenure within the overall system of land tenure. Feudal superiorities and feu duties are defining characteristics of feudalism and abolishing them would be historic after so many centuries. However, the overall system would continue to have a legacy of many aspects that are still essentially feudal in character (including the types of burdens and conditions land owners would still be able to impose on land they sell).

The SLC's 1991 proposals were very much in the mould of the 1970s' land tenure legislation. They continued the approach of clearing away some of the more conspicuous surviving elements of feudalism. They also maintained a narrow, technical focus on matters related to *conveyancing* – the arrangements governing the transfer of property in land. This focus can be justified by the conspicuous burden of the existing system. The abolition of feudal tenure should, for example, make the title deeds by which land is held substantially shorter and more straightforward and so more readily dealt with. This would make conveyancing easier, quicker and cheaper for everyone buying and selling houses or other properties. Given the thousands of property transactions made every year, the changes would bring widespread economic and social benefits.

Undue concentration on conveyancing concerns could, however, also be seen as a long-standing bias in the way land tenure matters have been considered by the legal profession in Scotland.[13] This bias was noted by Sir John Rankine in the 19th century in the first edition of his classic *The Laws of Land Ownership in Scotland* (1879), and it has been reinforced since then, even to the point where some lawyers tend to see land tenure as a part of conveyancing rather than the other way round.[14]

This concentration on conveyancing might also be seen as an urban bias. However, any reformed system has to be able to address the different demands on land tenure right across the land, from city centres to remote rural areas. The reform process should work down from the broad purposes and principles that underpin the land tenure system and not start from the relatively narrow concerns of conveyancing. The lack of this broader perspective in the work of the SLC is reflected by the fact that the committee they appointed in 1997 to advise the SLC on feudal reform consisted of Scotland's three Professors of Conveyancing and a solicitor from each of Scotland's four main cities.

The official commitment to replace feudal tenure was based originally on the need to remove some of its surviving anachronisms and to streamline conveyancing. The SLC has continued working on that agenda of legalistic changes. Thus, while their proposal to abolish feudalism has a promising sound to it to most people, the removal of feu duties (which can already be redeemed) and of superiorities (but retaining a similar system of private burdens) will not produce conspicuous changes. There is a danger of a mis-match between public expectations and what the SLC means by its claims to be replacing feudalism.

Requirement for Wider Reforms

Both the case for land tenure reform and the momentum to tackle it have already moved beyond the tasks the SLC has had in hand. Over and above removing specific feudal anachronisms, there is also the need to sort out the conspicuous areas of uncertainty that have built up in such an ancient system (for example, the nature of the *regalia* as mentioned on page 13 above). There is a wider requirement still, however, to ensure that the system of land tenure in Scotland is designed to meet the contemporary economic, environmental and social needs of society into the next century.[15]

This wider agenda recognises the full scope of the land tenure system. It is not simply about conveyancing or about the relationships between private interests in land, such as those between superiors and vassals or landlord and tenants. Land tenure is a comprehensive property system that covers the whole territory of Scotland and involves both the public and private legal rights and interests in that land. It is a system that defines the relationship between society as a whole and those who own land.

CHAPTER TWO

Time for Reform

The Developing Debate

The land issue has a long history in Scotland. The traditional relationship between land and power meant that land ownership was a prominent issue in the 19th century and before.[1] What is unusual about Scotland compared to other European countries is that it is still such an active issue. The scale of public support and media interest when, in 1993 and 1997 respectively, the Assynt crofters and Eigg islanders bought the estates on which they live, demonstrated the land issue's continuing potency. As the government minister Lord Sewel recently observed: "Land is a defining issue for the people of Scotland".[2]

Scotland's archaic system of land tenure and concentrated pattern of land ownership can appear to many people as issues left over from the 19th century and, until recently, the land debate in Scotland also tended to have a distinctly 19th century feel to it. The debate remained highly polarised and was characterised as a dispute between crofters and landlords in the Highlands. Gradually during the last 20 years, however, and with increasing pace over recent years, the land debate in Scotland has been transformed into a contemporary and well-argued case for reform.

The publication of John McEwen's *Who Owns Scotland* in 1977 can be taken as the start of that change. McEwen himself was very much part of the old debate. He was 90 when his book first came out and had personal experience of the harshness of 19th century landlords in Highland Perthshire. At the same time, his answer to the continuing problem of land ownership, nationalisation of the land, also already appeared by the 1970s to come from an earlier age. However, his book provided a new focus for the land debate that has been maintained since and McEwen continues to have a presence in that debate. After he died in 1992, two days short of his 105th birthday, the annual McEwen Memorial Lectures on 'Land Tenure in Scotland' were established as a tribute to his life and work. These Lectures have been central to the development of current thinking on land reform in Scotland.[3] McEwen's influence was also reflected in Andy Wightman's book *Who Owns Scotland* not only re-using McEwen's title, but being dedicated to McEwen – as was *A Pattern of Landownership in Scotland*, the only major book on the topic in the 1980s.[4]

The substantial development in the analysis of the issues associated with land ownership in Scotland found in Wightman's book compared to McEwen's, is a good illustration of how the debate has progressed. Another symbol of this change is that, while McEwen and his land nationalisation were classic 'old Labour', New Labour nevertheless stood at the 1997 General Election with a manifesto commitment to land reform in Scotland.[5] The land issue is no longer an old Labour bogey about the appropriation of private property. Instead, private property is recognised as a crucial currency in a modern democracy and increasingly refined arguments have been developed around the need to modernise the system of land tenure to ensure it is supportive of economic development, social democracy and environmental stewardship.[6]

The debate has expanded beyond the disadvantaged position of remote rural communities to cover land ownership issues in both urban and rural Scotland. The Assynts and Eiggs are key symptoms and important symbols but only one part of a bigger picture. At the same time, concern at the poor standards of land use on some estates is now set in the wider context of the need to achieve a balance between public and private interests that promotes the sustainable management of all Scotland's natural resources.

It is no coincidence that the land debate has broadened and deepened and achieved greater prominence as the expectations of a Scottish Parliament have grown. In 1997, with the general election and referendum, the case for land reform became partnered by the prospect that significant changes were now a very real likelihood. This has fundamentally changed the nature of the land debate. With the 'why' in position and the 'how' arriving with the Scottish

Parliament, the core issue has become 'what' – what are the land reform changes that are actually required?

The absence of any prospect of significant land reform for so many years has meant that, despite the long-standing and widespread support in Scotland for reform, relatively little attention has been given to the changes being sought. The gap on this issue has only started to be tackled in the last few years, as reflected in the increasing number of commissions and committees set up to study the system of land ownership and management in Scotland. The government now has its own Land Reform Policy Group working on this to prepare proposals for the Scottish Parliament, as do other organisations and civic bodies such as the Convention of Scottish Local Authorities and the Church of Scotland.[7]

The Components of Land Reform

One result of the greater attention to land reform is the increasing awareness of its different components. The overall system of land ownership and management is a huge topic and one that needs to be broken down into parts to be manageable. From the point of view of reforms, there can be considered to be three main components:

(i) *Property law*: the Scots legal system of land tenure determining how land can be held and transferred and the property rights associated with it.

(ii) *Administrative law*: the wide range of parliamentary statutes that interact with the laws of land tenure (for example, legislation setting up government bodies, environmental legislation).

(iii) *Regulations and incentives*: the non-statutory arrangements used to promote or control the use of rights over land (for example, grants and licences).

These components can be seen as levels, with land tenure at the base providing a legal framework of property rights. Administrative law has to conform to that framework and the use of regulations and incentives has to fit in with both administrative and property law. Thus, while all these levels come within the scope of land reform and need to be pursued in an integrated fashion, it is the land tenure system that is the basic underlying template with which other factors interact.

Changes to some of the many factors that interact with the land tenure system, such as government policies and grants, can have a much more immediate and marked impact on land use than land tenure reforms.[8] However, as an increasing number of commentators have shown, the underlying influence of land tenure is crucial and fundamental land tenure reform is needed to provide the new foundations for any wider package of land reform in the Scottish Parliament.

A Historic Opportunity

It has long been clear that there would need to be a Scottish Parliament to tackle land reform in Scotland. At a straightforward practical level, only a Scottish Parliament will potentially have time for it. Land tenure in Scotland and much of the related administrative law is defined by Scots law and consists of many separate laws and legal topics. The pressure on time at Westminster has meant for many years that there has only been space in any year for a handful of Scottish acts to cover all Scottish legislative requirements. Therefore, at best, only isolated land reform measures would have been possible in the British Parliament.

Time will also be under pressure in the Scottish Parliament. Already, in the lead up to its establishment, different interest groups are preparing lists of issues they would like to see the Parliament deal with. However, there are a number of reasons why it is likely that the Parliament will, alongside key topics such as education and health, address land reform and address it an early stage. The government's commitment to have land reform proposals ready for the Parliament is clearly one reason, but this commitment to pragmatic reforms is itself based on wider symbolic reasons why land reform will be important to the Scottish Parliament. Prominent amongst these is the fact that the territory over which the new Parliament will have jurisdiction will, by definition, be exactly the same territory covered by Scotland's land tenure system. The authority of the Parliament and of the land tenure system over that territory both involve issues of sovereignty. The survival of Scotland's system of land tenure in Scots law has been a crucial refuge for key aspects of Scotland's sovereignty as a nation and, as explained later in this book, provides a unique area of law through which the new Parliament can express its own sovereignty.

These links were encapsulated in the title of the 1997 McEwen Lecture on Land Tenure by Professor David McCrone – *Land, Democracy and Culture in Scotland.* He highlighted the ambiguity of the word 'land' itself – Land with a capital 'L' standing for the nation and land with a small 'l' associated with the countryside.[9] This, underpinned by the place of land in Scotland's history, is part of the deep cultural appeal of the land issue in Scotland. For the new Parliament, there will be a strong attraction to tap into the public support represented by the 'Assynt and Eigg factor' and as a way of showing it means business.[10] For a new democracy, there will be powerful symbolism in abolishing feudalism at the millennium. Indeed, after the delivery of the Parliament itself, tackling land reform has become seen by many as the most symbolic issue for Scotland's future.[11]

The Scottish Parliament will, of course, need more than just reasons of symbolism and popularity to address land reform. However, it is the combination of these powerful forces with the sound economic, social and environmental arguments that have been made, that contributes to an extraordinary conjunction of factors for land reform.[12]

Distinctive Solutions

Scotland's historic chance to introduce a new system of land tenure is an unusual opportunity for a western democracy. Scotland could move from the position of being the last country with a feudal system to become the first with a progressive system effectively targeted to the requirements of the new millennium.

In tackling this task, the systems of other countries are a resource that Scotland can draw on, although whether they are the English or foreign systems, it is a matter of features to learn from rather than models to adopt. This is due to the historically and culturally contingent nature of land tenure in different countries – each system has evolved in its own distinctive circumstances and there is no 'best' system that can be carried across borders. Land tenure arrangements are not fixed and they can not be isolated from the factors that have influenced their evolution in different countries as they have changed or been changed to meet changing requirements.

In the same way, Scotland's system of land tenure has been determined by the particular circumstances of Scotland and always been different from those in other countries.[13] Right from the start, feudalism was adopted in a distinctive form in Scotland, coming later to Scotland than most countries and being fused with existing native arrangements.[14] This distinctiveness has been maintained throughout the system's subsequent evolution and land tenure remains the most distinct sector of Scots law. No other main component has survived so unaffected by British and UK law since the 1707 Treaty and Acts of Union. This is due not only to the obstacles to reform that have existed since the change to a Westminster Parliament, but also to the important and conservative links between land tenure and the constitutional basis of Scotland as a country.

The long continuity and distinctive nature of land tenure in Scotland represents a substantial body of knowledge and experience, incorporating many aspects of a positive Scots legal tradition. This tradition includes other ancient strands of land tenure over and above the explicitly feudal elements. For example, the survival of udal tenure in the Northern Isles is a legacy of the 15th century transfer of Shetland and Orkney from Norway to Scotland, while there has been the continuing legacy of Gaelic Forest Laws through crofting legislation. Both represent important traditions of indigenous occupation and native rights in land. They illustrate how, in overhauling land tenure in Scotland, there is both a need to maintain valued features of the current system and the scope for distinctive solutions adapted to Scotland's contemporary needs.

Evolutionary Reform

The Scottish Law Commission's claim that their proposals would amount to a new system of land tenure for Scotland might be judged over-ambitious. However, even with far more wide-ranging reforms, it is somewhat academic to argue whether the system is being reformed or replaced. At one level, there is potential advantage in making a clear break with the past by identifying the proposed reforms as introducing a new system. However, at another level, the full extent of the laws involved in Scotland's overall system of land tenure mean that even thorough modernisation and reform would still leave the majority of the system relatively unaffected. Indeed, the sheer scale and complexity of Scotland's existing system of land tenure, including its uncertainties in places, has of itself long acted as a deterrent to change.

Land tenure reform should therefore not be seen as inventing an entirely new system, even if the introduction of a 'new system' is being claimed. The apparently massive task of introducing a 'new system' is best approached as a *process* of reform, building on the elements to be retained. Land tenure reform, let alone land reform, is not a single issue to be dealt with by a single Act of Parliament. It is a major sector of interest. An evolutionary approach allows the different reform measures, some of which may need to be done in a series of stages or in the correct sequence with other measures, to be tackled in turn and integrated with each other. Already in the current debate, proposals for different elements of reform are at different stages of development, from initial consultation papers to draft legislation. Thus, as different issues are tackled and taken forward, both before and within the Scottish Parliament, they can add to the existing process and build up into a systematic *programme of land tenure reform*. Also, as this process gathers momentum, it will act as a stimulus to more informed thinking about the land issue. As a result, the further problems that should be dealt with, and their solutions, will become much clearer.

Establishing a legislative programme of land tenure reform will contrast starkly with the main way Scotland's land laws have evolved since Scotland last had a Parliament. Scots law is unusual because of the particularly heavy extent to which it has relied on the establishment of precedent – the decision of a court that becomes taken as a statement of the law as it stands. In Scotland's case, the existence of a legal system without a revising parliament has placed undue emphasis on precedence in the development of the law. The legacy of this is that the law on particular aspects of land tenure (and other topics) is often constrained by legal decisions made long ago in very different circumstances.

Legal proceedings need, in broad terms, to be based on precedent, not as a conservative restriction, but as the mechanism of a healthy evolving system. However, a programme of land tenure reform in the Scottish Parliament will allow a rationalisation of the results of the precedent-led approach in Scotland over such an extended period. Parliament is not constrained by precedent like the courts and has the opportunity to overturn precedent where it is now considered to have led down avenues that are no longer thought appropriate, and to escape the uncertainty on points of law which have become bogged down in a quagmire of legal arguments.

There is a fresh opportunity with land tenure reform in the Scottish Parliament to decide what is required on particular issues before legal precedent comes into play again as an important way in which the land tenure system evolves and adapts.

An Understandable System

The rationalisation of the accumulation of legal precedent would assist one of the principles that should guide land tenure reform – making the system more straightforward and understandable and thus both more accessible and economically efficient.

The removal of feudal tenure is an obvious example. This would make conveyancing quicker and cheaper, because title deeds to properties could be shorter and simpler. They should also be more understandable. At present, most people are sheltered from the lengthy and obscure language of title deeds by their lawyers. A new system of titles in plain English would make these documents accessible to their owners. However, the objective of a more understandable system should also apply to the modernisation of land tenure in Scotland more generally, not just conveyancing. In part, this is simply a matter of language. The existing system has a heavy legacy of Latin and other archaic terms that could be replaced with more straightforward, understandable English. This need not result in any loss of the precision required of legal terms.

The need for the system to be readily understandable also extends beyond language. While a new system may, for example, have a new name for the *regalia* (the rights held by the Crown), it should also be based on a reasonably clear understanding of what these rights are. At the moment, this is not the case. Thus, the reform of land tenure would provide a wider opportunity for clarification and with it, reinvigoration of key concepts. This could also be linked to greater codification of different types of rights and the development of a more explicit overall framework and internal structure to the system.[15] These types of modernisation would help give the system a new practical and theoretical coherence. They would thus contribute to the operational effectiveness of a 'new system'.

A Unified Pattern

Another rationalisation that would make the system of land tenure in Scotland more straightforward and understandable would be the introduction of a unified pattern across the whole of Scotland for the way that land is held.

The present land tenure arrangements in Scotland are a single system in that, ultimately, all land is held either by, under or from the Crown under Scots law and constitutional conventions. However, within that, land can be held in a variety of ways, many of them archaic. These types of tenurial relationships are often classified as either direct from the Crown (allodial) or indirect (feudal). However, the distinction is not always clear. Titles held direct from the Crown can, for example, be feudal if they derive from the Crown's identity as the Paramount Superior. That there can be differences between legal authorities in the classification of tenures in Scotland is indicative of the state of the current system.

A number of different types of tenure have been abolished over the centuries and the final end to feudal superiorities should remove the complex patterns of rights and interests associated with them.[16] However, a number of different types of tenure would still be left. Some of these are obscure and extensive research was carried out for the Scottish Law Commission to try and identify them.[17] In addition to the udal tenure that survives in the Northern Isles, other more unusual examples include the *kindly tenants* of Lochmaben and *box tenure* in Paisley. There are also other types that have arisen due to particular circumstances (for example, the arrangements established under some of the 19th century Railway Acts for owning land covered by the railways lines).

The reform and modernisation of land tenure would enable all these various types of tenure to be replaced and all land would become held under one straightforward arrangement. In this way, a 'new system' would provide the opportunity to achieve an integrity and parity in the basic way land is held in Scotland. However, a unified system should not be seen as a uniform one. There would still be flexibility to reflect distinctive cultural traditions (for example, in the Northern Isles) and to have different arrangements governing the ownership of land in particular circumstances or for particular purposes (for example, housing restricted to particular uses).

Conditional Ownership

The replacement of feudal tenure and other less common forms of tenure with a new unified system raises important issues about the basic nature of this new form of tenure. The legal committees of conveyancing lawyers that examined feudal reform in the 1960s and 1970s, and since them the Scottish Law Commission, have proposed the introduction of what they call a system of *absolute ownership*. While *absolute* is used as a conventional legal term to describe a system where land is not held under either the Paramount Superior or other superiors, it is an archaic and misleading term for modern use. Ownership in a new direct system of land tenure would, as under the existing system, be *conditional* and should be described in terms that reflect that.

The conditional nature of the existing system is shown in the traditional representation that land owners (title holders) can do what they like with their land, subject to the terms of their title to that land and to the general laws of the country. Both these factors would still need to operate under a new system, even though the influence of titles would be significantly changed by the removal of feudal superiorities and related feudal features. Historically, when there were relatively few statutes, an owner's feudal title was the dominant influence. Over the centuries, there has been a long-standing trend of legislation to reduce the authority of superiors over their feudal vassals. However, the big change since the end of the 19th century has been the growth in the influence of statute law on the rights of title holders.

The limited evolution of the system of land tenure during the last hundred years and the increasingly rapid build up of legislation impacting on it, has continued with little regard to the relationship between these two influences. Land tenure reform would allow the tensions that have developed between titles to land and general statute law to be reconciled in a manner designed to balance the public and private interests they represent. These issues are explored later in this book, as the approach adopted to them will be crucial in influencing the outcome of land tenure reform. At this stage, it is important to recognise the part they play in the basic framework of Scotland's system of land tenure.

The abolition of feudal superiorities will profoundly alter the way land is owned in Scotland, but it will not create 'absolute' ownership in any normal sense of the word. At one level, without feudal superiors, land will be owned outright in the way that, for example, a bicycle is owned and a new owner will straightforwardly take over this ownership from the former owner. However, as explained in the next chapter, land is a different and distinct form of property in law and is classified, in contrast to bicycles and other forms of property, as 'immoveable property'. This label reflects the unique nature of land as property and, even without feudal superiors, all land will continue to be held subject to the rights and interests of others within the land tenure system. These can be seen as occurring at three levels relative to a land owner's rights – above (public rights), alongside (neighbours' rights) and below (tenants' rights).

The first of these levels (public rights) reflects that the ownership of land ultimately derives from the sovereign rights by which the territory of Scotland is held. These sovereign rights are held by the Crown and the ownership and use of land remains subject to the rights retained by the Crown in the public interest over all of Scotland's land (see Chapter 10). The second level ('alongside') recognises that an owner's use of their land is also conditional on the provisions within the land tenure system to safeguard the legitimate rights of neighbouring owners (see Chapter 13). These other owners thus have a legal interest in and over the owner's land. The third level ('below') reflects that an owner's use of their land is also conditional on the rights that any tenants have in that land. Land is the only form of property that can be leased under Scots law and, while tenants' rights derive from those of the owner, they also restrict the owner's rights during the tenancy (see Chapter 14).

   This framework, which forms a central part of the structure of land tenure in Scotland, can be represented as:

level of tenure:	*sovereignty*	*ownership*	*tenancy*
statutory holder:	*Crown*	*owner*	*tenant*
legal basis of holding:	*constitution*	*title deed*	*lease*

The nature of the rights and interests of these levels, including the potential influence of parliamentary statutes on them, are examined in detail in the chapters of sections 3 and 4. First, however, the next chapter explains more fully the distinctive nature of land as a form of property and the role of the tenure system in balancing public and private interests in land. Section 2 then describes how these interests are represented within the land tenure system. Particular attention is given to the Crown. This is not simply because of its fundamental position in land tenure, but because the question of what the Crown is often gives rise to confusion.

CHAPTER THREE

Towards a New System

Land and Property

The land tenure systems of different countries are based on the particular theories and definitions in those countries of land as a form of property. Historically, land has been of profound importance in wider theories about the place and role of property within societies. Scotland has been no exception to this.

Scotland's feudal system was based during its earlier centuries on the link between land ownership and jurisdiction and thus there was a high level of coincidence between the ownership of land and power in society. By the 17th and 18th centuries, this was being replaced by the concept of land as a commodity and source of wealth. Such ideas were also linked to the emergence of wider theories about land, labour and capital. A milestone in these developments in Scotland was the pioneering work of the distinguished Scots lawyer Stair in the 17th century. He provided the first coherent framework for the laws of Scotland, including property and lands laws, and his writing continues to be internationally cited as a classic text on property theory. Stair was followed in the 18th century by other Scots, such as Smith and Hume, who are also still widely quoted because of their major contributions to the development of thinking about the role of land and property in society.

The 17th and 18th centuries can be regarded as the beginning of the modern era of land ownership in Scotland. However, since that time, land as a form of property has become less significant in wider political theories. The development of modern industrialised societies has led to these theories concentrating on fuller interpretations of property (for example, intellectual property) and 'the means of production' (for example, a greater emphasis on the role of labour).[1]

An historical awareness of how the concept of property has

evolved and continues to evolve emphasises how land tenure systems reflect an underlying political philosophy about the relationship between land and society at any point in time.[2] In Scotland, the prospect of reforming its system of land tenure presents the opportunity and challenge of clarifying that philosophy and with it, the contemporary aims of the land tenure system. The present time is also a particularly interesting opportunity for such a review because of the new perspectives that have emerged over recent decades both on the role of property in modern democracies and on land as an environment resource. Private property has long been seen as an essential requirement of democracy.[3] However, more recently, it has become recognised much more fully as a vital currency in successful modern democratic economies. This has set the private ownership of land, as a form of private property, in a much more positive context. During the same period, the growth of environmental awareness has meant land is no longer viewed simply as a commodity, but as an ecological resource in which the public have a legitimate interest. The ownership of land is now seen by the general public as carrying an inherent responsibility for the sustainable management and stewardship of that land.

The traditional relationship between property and politics has made land ownership a sensitive issue in many societies in the past. However, in Scotland, the cultural importance still attached to the land issue means that it remains a very emotive topic despite the highly urban nature of contemporary Scottish society. Discussions of land ownership have tended to be unproductive as they polarise into those for or against the status quo. This has inhibited reasoned discussion of Scotland's system of land tenure. However, as has been observed by others,[4] the system of land tenure is too important a topic to neglect simply because of its proximity to political issues.

Scotland's system of land tenure, while it should reflect the values of contemporary society, is a technical system. It is a part of Scots law and within that, a part of Scots property law. Land tenure forms a distinct sector of property law because land has always been defined as a separate form of property.[5] This distinction between land and other forms of property in Scotland is based on definitions of *moveable* and *immoveable* property. Immoveable property consists of land and anything which is part of it. Trees in the ground, for example, are immoveable property, while felled timber is moveable property. The definition of land in this sense extends beyond just the physical natural resources of Scotland and associated natural processes. It includes buildings and anything else that might be considered to have become part of the land by accession. In these terms, land might be equated with the *cultural landscape* in its broadest terms – the product of natural and human influences over time.

The distinction between moveable and immoveable property is usually most familiar to people as the differences between fixtures (immoveable) and fittings (moveable). These factors arise between sellers and purchasers in house sales and between landlords and tenants in leases. However, the distinction also arises between heirs and executors under Scotland's laws of succession. The fact that the traditional label for immoveable property is *heritable property* points to the crucial importance, described later in Chapter 11, those laws have had in defining the differences between moveable and immoveable property.

The boundary between these two types of property is not always straightforward either in practice or in law, as the position has developed over time in Scots law in ways that are not necessarily clear or logical.[6] This can give rise to complex technical issues that might be dealt with by specialist lawyers during the modernisation and reform of Scotland's system of land tenure. The opportunity to rationalise the boundary between immoveable and moveable property could also be linked to codifying the types of *real rights* [7] that can exist in each of these types of property. However, the focus here is on the wider role and nature of the system of land tenure.

A Balance of Interests

Land tenure systems all start from the control that national sovereignty gives countries over their territory. The granting out of rights of ownership and use under that authority over parts of that territory is a normal feature of democratic political systems. The extent of rights granted and the terms and conditions of the grants varies between countries, so that private rights of land ownership are regulated to a lesser or greater degree. However, in each case, the system of private land ownership is a mechanism deployed in the public interest – or, in other words, the overall public interest, represented by parliament, uses private land ownership as part of the means by which the country's land tenure system operates.

Within this broad democratic arrangement, a relationship between public and private interests is inevitable and an overall purpose of land tenure systems is to deliver an acceptable balance.[8] Importantly, land tenure systems are a mechanism for delivering a balance, not the method of determining what the balance should be – a distinction between technical considerations and political considerations. It is the democratic process which determines the rights of ownership and use and the terms and conditions under which they are granted out and regulated. The democratic process therefore determines what the actual balance should be at any point in time and society has to adapt and change the system over time to ensure the system is best suited to delivering an appropriate balance for society's contemporary requirements and aspirations.

Thus, a system of land tenure simply provides a legal framework and is not concerned in the first instance with the pattern or distribution of land ownership and associated rights. There is, however, clearly an important relationship between the two. A conspicuous example is the connection between the major developments in the laws of land ownership in Scotland centred on the 17th century, and the trend towards fewer and larger-scale land owners that then continued well into the 19th century.

In most countries which have implemented new systems of land tenure during the last 50 years, the impetus has come from a commitment to wider programmes of land reform and has involved the three internationally recognised components: a new system of tenure; redistribution of property resources; and appropriate back-up or extension arrangements to implement and support the changes.[9] This pattern has been followed in many developing countries in Africa and elsewhere during the last 50 years to promote economic development and, during recent years, in former communist countries like Albania as they have converted to market economies.

In Scotland, by contrast, the official commitment to reform land tenure has yet to incorporate recognition of a need for redistribution. Here, the focus to date has been one of implementing a reformed system that refines the delivery mechanism. Some redistribution has to be considered inevitable in this process, otherwise no change would have occurred except in terminology. A conspicuous, if modest, example of 'redistribution' would be the abolition of superiorities, to the extent that it improves the rights of former vassals. Other examples will also arise from redefining and restating rights for a reformed system. The issues in each case are whether a change is justified in the overall public interest and whether, in the event of a reduction in private rights, compensation is due (see Chapter 6).

A land tenure system is a major democratic institution and can be regarded as a public interest system. In reforming the current system, it is important to recognise that feudal tenure does not, because of the retained rights of the Crown, make a separation at a technical level between public and private interests.[10] This is a feature not to be lost when replacing feudal tenure. The lack of distinct separation makes the system inherently conditional on the public interest and so makes it easier to achieve a genuine balance, rather than a compromise, between public and private interests.

Sustainability

While the purpose of land tenure systems in democratic societies is as a mechanism to facilitate an appropriate balance between public and private interests in land, the aim of this balance has itself to be seen as serving the overall public interest. The concept of the 'public interest', which equates to the national interest in an international context, is widely used and yet seldom defined. In Scotland, as elsewhere, there can be considered to be only one level of overall public interest, the interests of society as a whole. In theory, representations of the public interest in each of an endless array of specific issues are all presumed to add up to a complex, integrated whole. Inevitably this is more a concept than a reality, but the democratic process operates to resolve and represent the public interest and so define it in any particular context.

How is this overall public interest to be represented in land tenure? What are the guiding principles that reflect that interest and provide the system of land tenure with its sense of direction? These principles should be the same ones that underpin the democracy itself, reflecting the close relationship between the basic tenets of both democracy and property. Until recently, these might be considered to have been represented by the United Nations and European Charters on Human Rights developed after the Second World War.[11] These provide a natural justice or common good philosophy that is apolitical in its fundamental standing and the basis of a consensus within society over minimum acceptable standards.

More recently, this common good philosophy has expanded into the more holistic philosophy of sustainable development or 'sustainability'. This goes beyond the perspective of the international Human Rights charters by incorporating the relationships of societies with their environment and the environments of others. Like democracy, sustainability is a symbolic word and an abstract concept and is taken to represent this common good philosophy. It is again apolitical – as reflected, for example, by the international endorsement of sustainability at UNCED (the United Nations Rio Earth Summit 1992) and the subsequent adoption of it as official UK government policy.[12] The principles of sustainability were elaborated by the UNCED process and have continued to be developed since. Like all value systems, the pursuit of sustainability is interpreted as a coincidence of self interest and moral imperative. It is a positive philosophy on the way forward, rather than simply a code of constraint on actions that are no longer considered acceptable. While there are many issues to debate about sustainability, they tend to involve matters of interpretation, rather than questioning commitment to the principles themselves.

The holistic approach of sustainability involves all social, economic and environmental considerations, including the relationships between them. The concept has evolved from earlier ideas and, while few knew the word before the 1990s, sustainability has come to symbolise a cultural shift in 'world view' that is rapidly being absorbed by political and social institutions in the UK and elsewhere. Now, even if another word should come to replace sustainability, the philosophy it represents is, like human rights, here to stay as a guide to society's direction. A sense of the broad thrust of sustainability in the context of land tenure in Scotland can be represented by the following two statements adapted from official documents agreed at UNCED. The aim should be to ensure . . .

. . . The land and natural resources of Scotland are sustainably managed to meet the social, economic, ecological, cultural and spiritual needs of present and future generations.

. . . The stewardship and use of Scotland's natural resources in ways, and at rates, that maintain and enhance their biodiversity, productivity, regeneration capacity, vitality and their potential to fulfil, now and in the future, the relevant ecological, economic and social functions, at local, national and global levels and that does not cause damage to other ecosystems.

The concepts of sustainability and land tenure fit together relatively easily. Both are based on inter-generational concerns about the safeguarding and wise use of natural resources. Both are focused on relationships and balances. Both in the final analysis are about the relationship of people and place, whether at a site specific level or the level of a country and its population, or humankind and the Earth, now and in the future.

The broad principles of sustainability can only be defined in detail in the context of specific issues, when different courses of action can be assessed relative to each other (for example, determining the most sustainable form of electricity generation from a range of options).[13] For a new system of land tenure, sustainability provides a basic yardstick (like democracy and human rights) against which to measure arrangements. It provides a sense of direction to land tenure's overall purpose of balancing public and private interests in the management and use of land and natural resources.

Sustainability can be considered as a modern representation of the ideals of the more traditional idea of 'stewardship'. It shares the inter-generational commitment to sustainable management and the wise use of resources. Stewardship also symbolises the sense of responsibility that has long been taken in Scotland as part of the ownership of land. In the past, this responsibility was seen very largely in terms of private interests. It is now generally recognised, however, that the concept of stewardship encompasses both public and private interests.

Conclusions from Section 1

Chapter 1 Scotland's Feudal System

- It is no coincidence that Scotland is both the only country with a feudal system of land tenure and the country with the most concentrated pattern of large-scale private land ownership.
- Many elements of Scotland's system of land tenure are like the pattern of land ownership, in that they owe more to past circumstances and events than they do to recent trends and contemporary requirements.
- Narrowly focused proposals to remove the characteristically feudal elements of the system of land tenure in Scotland, now need to be broadened into a thorough modernisation and reform of Scotland's whole system of land tenure.

Chapter 2 Time for Reform

- There have been major developments in the debate about land tenure reform and the special significance of the issue makes it likely that it will be addressed by the Scottish Parliament at an early stage.
- Land tenure is a wide ranging issue involving many different specific topics and it will need to be tackled through a series of measures in an ongoing programme of land tenure reform in the Scottish Parliament.
- The modernisation and reform of the existing system of land tenure should produce a straightforward and unified system that also underpins the conditional nature of land ownership in Scotland.

Chapter 3 Towards a New System

- Land has always been treated as a separate form of property because of both its different physical character and special political significance and this has made land tenure a distinct sector of Scots law.

- The basic purpose of the land tenure system is to provide a legal framework that supports the balance of public and private interests in land that is judged appropriate by the wider democratic process at any point in time.
- The aim of the land tenure system in serving the overall public interest can be taken to be represented by the common good philosophy of sustainability, encompassing economic development, social democracy and environmental stewardship.

SECTION TWO
The Nature of Land Ownership

CHAPTER FOUR

The Involvement of the Crown

Constitutional Background

Sovereignty is essentially territorial: it is the supreme or ultimate power or authority over a certain territory. In Scotland's case that territory comprises all those areas over which the Court of Session and High Court of Justiciary have exercised jurisdiction since and under the Articles of the Union of 1707.[1] Thus, the same legal definition of Scotland as a country that existed before the Union has persisted throughout the subsequent period of incorporation in Great Britain (or the United Kingdom since the Union with Ireland Act 1800).

The sovereignty of the United Kingdom, as a 'limited' or 'constitutional' monarchy, is vested in the Crown. The Crown is represented by the monarch (the king or queen), who is the Sovereign for the time being. This position is uninterrupted as, under constitutional convention, the heir to the monarch succeeds instantaneously at the end of each monarch's reign.

The nature of the UK's sovereignty and the position of the Crown as Sovereign are part of constitutional law. However, their representation and interpretation are often not clear. There is no written constitution and most constitutional law is in fact governed by 'conventions' rather than laws. These conventions, which arise and lapse over time in no set way, are practices without legal force but which are treated as binding. Within this loosely defined situation, it becomes difficult to distinguish constitutional principles from political theories or philosophies of state and society.[2] However, in this context, constitutional law can be defined as concerned with the major rules and broad principles related to the institutions, procedures and practices involved in the government of sovereign nations. It can be distinguished from administrative law, which is concerned with the detail and application of these matters.[3]

Within the constitutions of modern democracies, state power and individual liberty are seen as inseparable: "the rights of the state are in a sense nothing but the communal rights of the individuals who make up the state".[4] The central concern of constitutional law is the balance or limits between these two interests and the means by which they are maintained. This balance at the constitutional level sets the context within which land tenure serves as a mechanism to balance public and private interests.

Within the British constitution, the Crown's special position and sovereign powers are described by a body of rules, principles and doctrines and known as the Royal prerogative.[5] These powers reflect the Crown's position as the 'constitutional repository' of the powers or necessary incidents of sovereignty that have not been not superseded by parliamentary statutes. They are not a clearly delineated set of powers and can be classified in a number of ways. They can be divided, for example, into personal prerogatives (such as certain immunities from the law and conferring certain chivalrous honours) and the prerogatives related to the three main constitutional divisions of power: executive (such as the authority to enter treaties and declare war); legislative (such as the authority to summon and dissolve parliament); and judicial (such as the authority to initiate and abandon legal proceedings).[6]

A specific sub-category of the Royal prerogative is the Crown's special property rights, known in Scots law as the *regalia majora* and *regalia minora*. These property rights adhere to the Crown as Sovereign. However, the historical basis of the Crown's special legal position derives from its position in the feudal system. Thus, these prerogative powers are of feudal origin in Scotland and developed from the time when the ownership of property included powers of legal jurisdiction within that property. A reformed system of land tenure for Scotland would need to be based on contemporary interpretations of the constitutional position of the Crown, and particularly its special property rights, in Scots law.

National Sovereignty

Scotland is considered to have become a united country in the 9th century and continued as an independent sovereign nation state for over 800 years, until the Treaty of Union with England of 1707. The personal union of the Crowns of these two nations in 1603 did not impinge directly on their statehood, although concerns about divergent succession laws were an important factor in England promoting the Union of 1707.

The Treaty of Union of 1707, with its XXV Articles, was adopted by Acts of Union in exactly the same terms in both the Scots and English Parliaments. Under the Articles, Scotland and England both ceased to exist as independent states and were replaced by the single state of Great Britain. The Parliaments were replaced by the first Parliament of Great Britain. This became the Parliament of the United Kingdom following the Union with Ireland Act of 1800, and the current Parliament (March 1998) is the 52nd of the United Kingdom.

The Articles of Union distinguished between provisions that might be altered by the new parliament and those that could not be changed (they were to be settled for "all time coming"). Certain changes in the law since, however, can be considered contrary to the intention that particular provisions should be immutable. As a result of those and of wider changes over time, the status of some of the provisions in the Articles is uncertain. History and legal precedent can provide a clearer guide to the current situation than some of the Articles themselves. However, the Articles of Union continue to be a live legal document of profound constitutional significance.[7]

Under the Articles of Union, Scotland surrendered its independent statehood, but continued to be a sovereign nation. The status of Scotland as a stateless nation is fairly unusual internationally and has attracted particular sociological and political study.[8] There has also been a significant growth of interest over recent decades in the autonomy of Scottish constitutional law. It is well established through the Scottish Courts that, although the Acts of Union created a unified Crown, they did not harmonise the Crown's special constitutional and legal positions in the jurisdictions of Scotland and England. In Scotland, it is Scots law that defines prerogatives and immunities and determines matters such as, for example, how the Crown may acquire property or make contracts.[9] Thus, while the prerogatives may not be clearly defined in either jurisdiction, differences are clear and it is anticipated that recognition of these will increase over time (for example, under the influence of the Scottish

Parliament). There has been, and continues to be, an erosion of distinctive Scottish positions due to a range of factors, such as the harmonising impact of much contemporary British legislation or the use of English precedent in Scottish legal cases that go to the House of Lords. At a general level, Scots law has been more 'sceptical' of claims of Crown prerogative, reflecting broader differences of tradition in the two jurisdictions.[10]

Historically, some of the important constitutional differences between Scotland and England are reflected in the Bill of Rights passed by the English Parliament in 1688 and the Claim of Right passed by the Scots Parliament in 1689. These two pieces of legislation, though now much superseded, remain of considerable constitutional significance in the absence of a written constitution or the enactment of any more contemporary Claim/Bill of Rights.

The Acts of 1688 and 1689 illustrate the fundamental difference between the Crown's sovereignty in the two jurisdictions, based on the nature or identity of the Crown as determined by the respective sources or authority of its sovereignty. The difference is also demonstrated in the different style of monarch's titles in each kingdom pre-Union. In England, the monarch was the King or Queen of England. In Scotland, the monarch was always the King or Queen of Scots (for example, Mary, Queen of Scots). This difference reflects that in Scotland, in a basic contrast with the English position, sovereignty still derives from the people.[11] The Crown's identity in Scotland is dependent on the sovereignty of the people and the Crown's status is as the representative of the people or, as traditionally identified, the *Community of the Realm*.

Following the Union of 1707 and the subsequent changes in relation to Ireland, the current style and title of the Sovereign or Crown is ' . . . of the United Kingdom of Great Britain and Northern Ireland'. The nature of the sovereignty in each country has not changed, however, and in Scotland continues to be based on the sovereignty of the people. Recent documents articulating this include The Claim of Right produced in 1988 by the Constitutional Convention for a Scottish Parliament and the draft Constitution for Scotland by Professor Neil MacCormick published in 1991.[12] The first of the six Articles of that constitution asserts in its first sentence: "The right of the people of Scotland . . . to sovereignty over the territory and natural resources of Scotland is full and unqualified". The distinctive nature of that sovereignty and associated prerogatives in Scotland, including the existing status of the Sovereign in Scotland as Paramount Superior, all provide the starting point for any reform of the system of land tenure in Scotland.

Community of the Realm

The constitutional principle in Scotland of the Crown as representing the Community of the Realm has a long pedigree. The Community of the Realm emerged in the late 13th century as a concept that represented the constitutional integrity of the Kingdom of Scotland. At the time, it formed the basis of a pioneering and practical expression in a European context of national sovereignty based on the sovereignty of the people.[13] An eloquent statement of this from that period is the internationally renowned Declaration of Arbroath (1320).

The Community of the Realm was an abstract idea and, unlike the uses of similar terms in England at the time, was not and did not become associated with particular groups (for example, the feudal baronage or 'the commons' in England). It comprehended "the Whole Community of the Kingdom" as an early expression of the later concept of a nation or a national state.[14] This contrast with the English position is reflected over subsequent centuries in the different development in the two countries of the relationships between Crown and subjects and parliament. The respective late 17th century Claim of Right and Bill of Rights are summary representations of the continuing contrast and, in particular, the emerging English view on the supremacy of parliament. The Union since 1707 has tended to make the differences less apparent, but the contrast continues to be reflected in, for example, contemporary legal authority that "the principle of the unlimited sovereignty of Parliament is a distinctly English principle which has no counterpart in Scottish constitutional law".[15]

The early link between the Crown and the Community of the Realm in Scotland had a crucial bearing on the concept of the Crown as Paramount Superior. Conventional feudal theory and practice was based (in England and elsewhere) on the premise that a kingdom was first and foremost a feudal entity and in that sense, the property of its king or queen. In Scotland's feudal system, this situation was radically tempered by the Crown's status as representative of the Community of the Realm, which vested that 'ownership' in the sovereignty of the people. This was reinforced at the time by the institution of guardianship and the political and constitutional significance this achieved in Scotland at a national level (for example, William Wallace as the Guardian of Scotland), rather than its usual narrow role with individual feudal properties (when a guardian would be appointed to look after the property until, for example, the heir came of age).[16]

These historical and constitutional considerations have a direct bearing on the identity of the Crown in any reformed system of land tenure for Scotland. The abolition of feudal tenure would remove the Crown's position as Paramount Superior, and so the Crown's identity in a new system would need to be clarified. The starting point is that the Crown's identity would be based on representing the Community of the Realm. This accords not only with constitutional principle, but with contemporary expression of the overall public interest in the ownership and management of Scotland's territory and natural resources.

Names and Titles

In a reformed system of land tenure, the Crown's feudal label of Paramount Superior would no longer be appropriate. However, the Crown would still have an important position in a new system of land tenure. This would remain one of the Crown's relatively distinct identities and there would be utility in continuing to give this identity its own name. Any new label should convey a greater sense of trusteeship and guardianship, to reflect the Crown's role as representing the Community of the Realm. A new name should also, ideally, reflect indigenous cultural traditions, while not carrying inappropriate historical associations. The Crown could, for example, adopt the existing royal title of Steward of Scotland (Steward or Seneschal and in Gaelic, Ard-Stiubhard).[17] The connotation of stewardship would match the Crown's overall responsibilities within land tenure.

The title of 'Prince and (Great) Steward of Scotland' has been held by the Sovereign's eldest son since the 14th century. The title Prince does not relate to the whole of Scotland but the 'Principality of Scotland', being lands in Renfrew and the Stewartry appropriated as the patrimony of the Sovereign's eldest son for his maintenance. The title and revenues of the Principality are held by the Sovereign when the Sovereign has no son.[18] With the abolition of feudal tenure, the superiority of the Sovereign's heir would no longer exist over the lands of the Principality. It might be presumed that the concept of the principality would also lapse at that point and with it, the redundant feudal titles. The title 'Steward of Scotland' could then be reconstituted for the Crown's identity in Scotland's reformed land tenure system.

The fate of the title 'Prince of Scotland' illustrates the wider issue of the link between feudal title deeds to land and aristocratic and related titles. With a new, non-feudal system of land tenure, this linkage could be broken and such titles either lapse or become honorary titles not dependent on or associated with holding particular lands. A conspicuous example is *Baronies*, which are the highest feudal grant because of the powers they used to convey to their holders (for example, holding local courts). Around 2000 Barony titles may still exist in Scotland.[19] A feudal Barony title is inseparable from land under current law and inconsistent with a non-feudal system. They could be replaced with conventional title deeds, and with this, the concept of Scotland's feudal barons extinguished.

The distinction between titles (royal, aristocratic and related) that are a part of feudal tenure and similar titles that are simply honorary or chivalrous, is not always clear. Prince Charles, as the Sovereign's eldest son, includes amongst his titles Earl of Carrick and Baron of Renfrew. The former was created as a title by Act of Parliament, while the latter is feudal title rather than a lordship of Parliament or peerage title. Thus, a distinction has to be made between reforms as a result of changing the system of land tenure and what would be more properly associated with reform of the House of Lords and hereditary titles generally. While many such hereditary titles (for example, Duke and Earl) were based on land and feudal identity, there is no necessary connection now.

Much of this is closely connected to the Royal Family. In the first instance, the monarch is still considered feudal both in England and in most other European monarchies. This is because, despite conversion to non-feudal land tenure systems, specific provision has not been made to convert the monarch to a post-feudal status or identity.[20] Addressing this in the Scottish situation might also be linked to removing the option for monarchs, on succession to the throne, to choose the revenues of Crown lands rather than adoption of the Civil List as a source of income.

Amongst the 'Officers of the Crown' and within the 'Offices of the Royal Household', there are hereditary positions that are considered as heritable property and can be recorded in the Register of Sasines.[21] In particular, many of these were and some still are, linked to feudal landed estates. Amongst the Officers of the Crown, for example, the Lord High Constable (Earls of Erroll) and The Earl Marischal (capable of being revived) and within the Royal Household, the Master Carver (Barony of Anstruther), the Poulterer (Barony of Dean) and the hereditary Keepers of Royal palaces and castles.

The abolition of feudal tenure could break the link between these positions and land. Wider issues are involved in whether they and the range of other hereditary posts in the Royal Household should continue to be heritable. Most have little or no direct political significance, except at coronations and other special Royal occasions. However, since the last century, a few such posts have been converted to honorary, non-hereditary appointments by the Secretary of State (for example, The Knight Marischal and Keeper of Dumbarton Castle) or else become appointments based on merit (for example, the Historiographer Royal). This provides an option for posts, heritable and non-heritable, that might be retained.

In such reforms, a distinction has to be drawn between the removal of archaic and anomalous positions and honours and the need to protect institutions that represent significant parts of Scotland's national identity and constitutional apparatus. Amongst these are many public appointments related to government and the courts in which the Crown's role is purely symbolic.

CHAPTER FIVE

The Underlying Framework

This chapter considers the relationship in Scotland's system of land tenure between the Crown's sovereign rights, the authority of Parliament and the definition of land ownership as holding a valid title to land.

Ultimate Ownership

Sovereign authority over the territory of Scotland is vested in the Crown and this confers on the Crown the 'ultimate ownership', as it is traditionally expressed, of that territory. However, in the contemporary world, neither sovereign authority nor ultimate ownership can be seen in such absolute terms as formerly. The nature of the relationships that now exist between and within states mean that sovereignty, for instance, can be 'external' and 'internal' and have both political and legal forms.[1]

The external sovereignty of a state has become significantly modified by the development and increased standing of international law. The issues involved are perhaps exemplified for the UK in its relationship with the European Union. The UK Parliament, unconstrained by a written constitution or fundamental law, still superficially follows the doctrine of its own supremacy and capacity to make or unmake any law. However, it is now recognised that, for example, some of its laws can not in reality be unmade (for example, those granting independence to former dominions). Also, even where international agreements such as the European Convention on Human Rights have not yet been given legal force in the UK by parliamentary enactment, they are adhered to by 'the presumptions of procedural convention' or rules that govern Parliament.[2]

The nature of external sovereignty directly affects the scope and character of laws of land tenure. Notions, for example, of the extent of sovereignty in the airspace over a territory continue to be altered by developments in technology and communications. The extension by states through international agreements of specified rights of sovereignty into international waters beyond the defined territorial waters previously claimed, also illustrates the porous nature of territory (see Chapter 7).

Issues of internal sovereignty arise between the component parts of a nation state, for example, in federal systems such as Germany or the USA. They also arise between the interlocking levels and forms of sovereignty found in the UK (as illustrated by the legislation for the Scottish Parliament). In turn, issues of internal and external sovereignty demonstrate the relative nature of the idea of 'ultimate ownership'.

In legal theory, under the present feudal system, the Crown's 'ultimate ownership' of Scotland derives from God. In tenurial terms, the Crown, representing the Community of the Realm, holds Scotland from God. As part of this, all the lands of Earth are seen as held from God. This ancient view of the Crown as one of God's tenants-in-chief responsible for looking after part of the Earth can be linked to modern global concern for the sustainable management of natural resources. However, in a reformed secular system of land tenure for Scotland, the Crown's position could be based straightforwardly on its sovereignty under constitutional law without recourse to religious theory.

At the same time, the end of feudal tenure would allow the identity of the Crown as Paramount Superior to be absorbed into the Crown as Sovereign. The two words sovereign and superior in fact share the same linguistic derivation. Abolition of the position of Paramount Superior would consolidate the fact that the Crown's fundamental position in land tenure is a matter of *rights of sovereignty*, rather than *rights of property* per se.[3] The basis of sovereignty makes it clearer that the notion of 'ultimate ownership' is itself not about ownership as such. The Crown holds all land on the basis of its sovereignty and thus holds it in trust for the public and on behalf of the overall public interest. The Crown's position can be represented as the *source* of all ownership, with ownership equating with holding a title deed to land. The Crown, through its sovereignty, requires no title.

In a reformed system of land tenure, as at present, ownership of

certain parts of the territory and of certain rights over all the territory, would never be granted out. They would be held constitutionally by the Crown inalienably in trust for the public (see Section 3).
Other parts and other rights can be, and in part have been, granted
out from the Crown and are 'owned' by others by virtue of holding
a title deed. These tiltleholders include both public owners (the state
as represented by the government and government bodies) and
private owners (as represented by the types of natural and legal
persons defined as able to hold titles to land).

Thus the Crown retains a stake or legal interest in all land. There
are therefore rights held on behalf of the public interest in the land
of all owners, whether the owner or titleholder is the state or a
private person. There is thus both a general public interest in having
a system of private property and also a public interest retained in the
actual private property itself. That retained public interest is
stronger in Scotland than in comparable countries because of the
survival of feudalism and the more substantial stake that system
gives the Crown as Paramount Superior in the lands of its vassals.
This public interest needs to be clarified and consolidated to underpin the balance of presumption between public and private interests
in a reformed system of land tenure.

Democratic Sanction

While *national sovereignty* can be considered to derive from the
sovereignty of the people and to be represented by the *Crown as
Sovereign*, this constitutional equation is dependent on the fourth
pillar of sovereignty, the *sovereignty of Parliament*. The Crown and
Parliament are both representations of the public interest in Britain's
democratic constitutional monarchy.

The changing relationship between the Crown and Parliament
over the centuries has been a central theme in the evolution of the
British constitution. The 17th century was the watershed, represented by the Scots Parliament's Claim of Right (1689) and English
Parliament's Bill of Rights (1688), in the assertion of the authority
of both Parliaments (and the subsequent British Parliament) over the
Crown or Royal power. Any of the Crown's prerogative powers,
together with related rights pertaining to the Crown (for example,
succession), can be changed, reduced or removed by Parliament. The

Crown's prerogative powers can not, technically, be expanded by Parliament, following the doctrine that they are residual powers and superseded by statute. However, the prerogative can 'expand' through reinterpretation and the lack of precision with which prerogative powers have been defined at any time, has enabled them to have a measure of adaptability to changing circumstances.[4]

Despite the control of Parliament over the Crown through the constitution, the Crown also has constitutional authority over Parliament (for example, in the power to summon and dissolve Parliaments). In this ambiguous situation, the Crown can be considered as an abstract but permanent representation of the public interest or sovereignty of the people, while Parliament is a contemporary expression of it at any point in time. The contrast is similar to the difference between the relatively permanent theory of democracy and the reality of actual democratic practices at any particular time (for example, the major changes in the franchise in Britain over the last 100 years).

The Crown's position 'in Parliament' is paralleled by its position 'in land'. The notion of the Crown's 'ultimate ownership', dependent on sovereignty and prerogative, goes beyond Parliament but is regulated by Parliament. There is essentially no difference in this constitutional relationship in Scotland whether it is through the United Kingdom Parliament or, in future, the Scottish Parliament. The Scottish Parliament will be an improved representation of democracy and it might be considered that the Parliament will be more likely to legislate on Scots land law than a United Kingdom Parliament. It might also reach some different conclusions in such legislation.

The concepts of nation, state and government are intimately connected. While a nation can be seen as the people and/or its territory, so 'state' can be used to refer to either the body politic controlling government or the place itself (hence the shared derivation with 'estate'). Government can also be either the act of governing or the government itself (the collective term for those doing the governing). In these terms, a nation's sovereignty is formalised as 'the state' and implemented by 'the government'. Scotland is ambiguously positioned as a stateless nation, but has been described as a 'semi-state' because of its relatively high level of autonomy.[5] This political autonomy has also been gradually increasing over recent years and is, of course, about to develop substantially with the establishment of the new Scottish Parliament.[6]

While the democratic sanction of the Westminster Parliament over the Crown is similar throughout Britain, this should not be allowed to obscure the different starting points of the relationship between the Crown and Parliament with respect to land tenure in Scotland and England (and Wales). In England, the Crown has virtually no status in land tenure, reflecting England's different constitutional and parliamentary history. This English model has been in the ascendancy through the UK Parliament. The Scottish Law Commission's 1991 land tenure proposals have perhaps promoted this model through their relative neglect in considering the position of the Crown.

In reforming land tenure in Scotland, it is important that the Crown's distinctive identity is retained and not lost or weakened, since this identity facilitates in broad terms a more constructive balance of public and private interests (including, for example, over the types of regulation of land owners' rights where compensation is or is not due, as explained more fully in Chapter 6). It would also allow a number of more specific issues to be resolved more easily. The difference of Royal prerogative in Scotland, together with the associated less sympathetic legal attitude towards the prerogative, could be used to dispense with, for example, some problems over the special treatment of Crown land (for example, the presumption that certain types of Crown land are not affected by Sites of Special Scientific Interest or other statutory designations unless specifically included in the relevant legislation).

Titleholding

The idea of 'ownership' is central to land tenure systems, but ownership is not a clear-cut concept and can be defined in varying terms in different systems. Over recent centuries, much of the momentum for the development of the concept of ownership in land tenure was as a reaction away from feudal systems. This development progressed to the extent that the concept of ownership came to be considered as incompatible with feudal tenure.[7] This was because feudal tenure, for example as it still survives in Scotland, retains a hierarchy of property interests in any particular piece of land in contrast to the more absolute notions of ownership that developed in England and many other countries.

Modern thought over recent decades, while still seeking to reduce the rights over an owner's land that can be held by other owners, has generally moved towards a more relative view of the rights of ownership.[8] This new perspective sees ownership as 'a bundle of rights' and recognises, crucially, that property rests in rights rather than land itself. These rights can each be defined as representing a valid claim against another or others under the laws governing the system of land tenure and the 'land' can be considered as the area or jurisdiction over which the rights pertain. However, the rights are limited, relative and conditional, reflecting the increasing influence of Parliamentary statutes in defining ownership and promoting moves away from more absolute 19th century notions.

However, not all rights or bundles of rights over land amount to ownership. Under Scotland's existing tenure, the rights of some feuars (owners) can be in many respects less than those of crofters (tenants). In the final analysis, the key distinction is a valid, written and recorded title to land. A land owner is someone who holds a valid title, while land ownership is defined simply as holding a title to land. Under a reformed system in Scotland, these titles would be held directly under the Crown's sovereign rights and guaranteed by the state once they had been recorded in the public register of titles to land.

Within this system, a title would be the only basis of ownership. In completing the systematic coverage of the map-based Land Register (see 5.4), it is likely that there will be areas to which no-one either has or can claim valid title.[9] As at present, these areas would automatically fall to the Crown. This can be seen as a logical result of the Crown's 'ultimate ownership' of all land, though no longer in terms of reversion to the superior under feudal theory. It can also be related to the laws of succession under which all property without heir passes to the Crown. This, in turn, reflects the deeply entrenched philosophy in Scots law that the people of Scotland are all ultimately related – *all Jock Tamson's bairns* (Burns), a philosophy that also links back to the concept of the Crown as representing the Community of the Realm.

In a new system of land tenure for Scotland, each new owner or titleholder would straightforwardly and directly replace the former titleholder as the land owner. The state already guarantees the titles on the Land Register, so removing the role of prescription in defining or confirming titles. Titles would derive from the former owner, but would not be held *from* the Crown or other superior in the sense that they are under the current feudal system. However, the title would not be free from the Crown, in that all titles to land would still be held under the Crown by virtue of the Crown's sovereign rights from which the land tenure system derives.

The essential nature of titles would not be any different whether the owner is the state itself or some other person. However, while there is a general need to define the natural and legal persons that can hold titles, there is also a particular need to draw a clear distinction in titleholding between the Crown and state. This arises from the use of powers of prerogative by (Her Majesty's) Government and the increasing lack of clarity over which bodies are covered by these powers. There is a less obvious distinction between public bodies and bodies outwith government now that some agencies have been made autonomous and others partially privatised.

Ownership can be straightforwardly equated with state guaranteed titles that can be held directly by persons (natural and legal, as defined). The title covers what is being conveyed by its former titleholder, but is held under the Crown and Parliament. This conveys to the titleholder, through the title, rights and responsibilities. The old adage has been that land owners can do what they like with their land subject to their title and statutory law. This has tended to underplay the recognition of public interest responsibilities and emphasise the sense of burdens already deriving from superiorities. Nevertheless, the adage should more accurately have been that land owners 'can *only* do . . .'.

The introduction of a reformed system of land tenure provides an opportunity to consolidate the public interest commitments in holding a title to land, while also promoting private interests by freeing them of the outdated burdens and intrusions of feudalism. These public interest commitments exist already and could be codified as part of a basic set of private rights and public responsibilities that would go with holding a title to land or land ownership (for example, see Chapter 10).

Record Keeping

A basic requirement of any modern system of land tenure is a method of recording who has what rights over what, in other words an official system for registering titles to land. Historically, Scotland was an early leader in such matters with the establishment of its Register of Sasines in 1617 as a written record of titles to land. This supplemented and subsequently replaced the ritual handing over of symbols of rights in land, for example earth and stones, between parties to mark changes in ownership. The now antiquated system of recording title deeds in the Register of Sasines is still in operation. However, since the Land Registration (Scotland) Act 1979, it is being gradually replaced by a new system that, when fully developed, refined and implemented, should form an adequate record upon which to base a modernised system of land tenure.

Starting with Lanarkshire in 1979, counties have been gradually brought within the scope of the Land Register (for example, Aberdeenshire in April 1996). The target is that all counties will be on the Register by 2003. Once a county is on the Register, all property transactions within it are recorded in a consistent form and defined on Ordinance Survey maps. All this data is computerised, allowing easy access to information and also open access to anyone at a commercial rate. The Land Register was one of the government's first Next Step agencies in Scotland and its operation is self-financing. Each year £1 is voted in Parliament to the Land Register as the way of maintaining government control over the agency.

It is estimated that there are around five million properties in Scotland (estimated from the number on the Register of Sasines, but the number of properties continues to grow, for example, through new housing). It is also estimated that 60% of Scotland's properties are in the counties already covered by the Land Register. However, individual properties are currently only entered into the Land Register at a transaction. Properties are estimated to change hands on average once every seven years and at present only an estimated 40% of properties in counties covered are so far on the Register.

There is scope to speed up the addition of counties to the Register by increasing the resources available for the task, for example, by higher charges for the use of the Register. However, legislation will be necessary to complete coverage by requiring the production of titles (or other demonstration of ownership such as prescription or occupation). The aim of comprehensive coverage could be linked to the introduction of Scotland's new system of land tenure.

The computerised map base of the Land Register also has the potential to be linked to other computer databases[10] and so, with the system of new titles, provide a systematic *cadastral* of the ownership and character of land in Scotland. The technology to put in place such a system already exists.

CHAPTER SIX

Public and Private Interests

The previous chapter outlined the basis of the public interest in land through Crown rights and the authority of Parliament. Against that background, this chapter considers the position of land ownership within a reformed system of land tenure and examines some of the main mechanisms that exist to balance public and private interests in land. These include Human Rights Conventions, compulsory purchase arrangements, the operation of the voluntary principle, the nature of statutory regulation and the requirements of a land tribunal system.

Peaceful Enjoyment

Establishing a reformed system of land tenure provides the opportunity to consolidate, clarify and improve the rights of titleholders (land owners) and of others with a legal share in those rights (for example, tenants and heirs). The most basic of these rights is security in their property, or what is termed the right of peaceful enjoyment.

The abolition of feudal tenure would improve the rights of the overwhelming majority of land owners in Scotland by removing the superiorities and associated rights and burdens held by others over their properties. As part of this, their security as land owners in their property would be improved by removing 'irritancy', the power under which a superior could resume a property because of a breach of the feudal conditions in the title to the property. Security will also be improved by the system of state guaranteed titles operated with the new Land Register for Scotland (see previous chapter).

The replacement of feudal tenure can promote the peaceful enjoyment of land owners generally by reducing or removing the intrusion of the property rights of other titleholders in their property (for example, a right of pre-emption that gives the previous owner an opportunity to buy the property back). What might be considered the genuine interests of other titleholders would still exist (for example, rights of servitude such as access to a water supply), while particular difficulties with titles would still be dealt with through the rational and democratically accountable procedures of the Lands Tribunal.

A wider requirement for titleholders is the right of reasonable security against actions of the state. While the influence of superiors over vassals has continued to be reduced this century, the influence of statutes and related state powers on private property rights has grown considerably.

Protection of the individual against the state (for example, the confiscation of property without due cause or compensation) is a matter of basic human rights and falls within the sphere of the European Convention on Human Rights (ECHR) and its associated Commission and Court. The UK is already a signatory to the Convention and the current government's proposal to incorporate it into domestic law by an Act of Parliament, would mean that the provisions of the ECHR relating to property would be fundamental legal principles in a reformed system of land tenure for Scotland.

The ECHR was first adopted in 1950. It elaborated on the UN Universal Declaration of Human Rights signed the year before. In the formulation of both, the right of property proved particularly sensitive.[1] While it was incorporated in the Universal Declaration as "Everyone has the right to own property alone as well as in association with others" (Art.17), it has been omitted altogether from subsequent United Nations Covenants that elaborate on the Declaration. The contentious nature of the debates on this right in the Council of Europe also meant that agreement was not reached in time to include it in the ECHR. However, it was incorporated 16 months later in March 1952 as Article 1 of the First Protocol in the form:

> Every natural or legal person is entitled to the peaceful enjoyment of his possessions. No one shall be deprived of his posses-

sions except in the public interest and subject to the conditions provided for by law and by the general principles of international law.

The preceding provision shall not, however, in any way impair the right of a State to enforce such laws as it deems necessary to control the use of property in accordance with the general interest or to secure the payment of taxes or other contributions or penalties.

Property is incorporated in the Article in a wider sense than just property in land and, indeed, most of the cases under the Article have related to other forms of property (for example, copyright). Possession is also a wider concept than ownership. It is possible to have ownership without possession and therefore to affect ownership without disturbing possession. At the same time, while there are other provisions in the ECHR that relate to landed property (for example, rights of privacy), enjoyment of the rights of possession and ownership are themselves subject to, or tempered by, all the ECHR's other provisions.

Most fundamentally, *peaceful enjoyment* is made subject to the *public or general interest*. The European Court of Human Rights has also recognised that in democratic societies "the notion of public interest is necessarily extensive . . ." and that the margin of discretion available to Parliaments is also very wide. In the 1986 case brought by the Trustees of the Duke of Westminster against the Leasehold Reform Act of 1967 for England, which allowed long leaseholders to buy the freehold of property at a low valuation, the Court was asked whether it was in the public interest to transfer property from one individual to another. The Court concluded:

> The taking of property in pursuance of a policy calculated to enhance social justice within the community can properly be described as being 'in the public interest'. (In Beddard, 1993)

This relationship in human rights conventions, with private rights conditional on the public interest, reflects the overall nature of the balance between public and private interests which should apply in any system of land tenure for Scotland.

Freedom and Quietness

The provisions of Article 1 of the ECHR's First Protocol, founded on the basic principle that safeguarding private property has to be seen within the context of the needs of the public interest, are consistent with legal tradition in Scotland. It has long been central to Scots land law that the private ownership of land is held subject to the public interest. The 19th century authority Erskine, for example, describes the "legal limitation" on private land that it "must give way to the public necessity or utility", as the "universal right in the public over property".[2]

While this universal public right derives from sovereignty, the powers associated with it (other than the Royal prerogative in times of war) have long been vested in Parliament. These powers have traditionally been seen as divided between those related to the compulsory purchase of property from land owners and those related to the regulation of the use of property by land owners.

Here, the balance between the public interest and 'peaceful enjoyment' can be considered a balance between, on the one hand, *compulsion and regulation* and, on the other, *freedom and quietness*. This again reflects a basic democratic presumption that land owners, as far as is possible compatible with the public interest, should have freedom from intrusion (for example, compulsory purchase) and disturbance (for example, additional regulation). The notion of 'freedom and quietness' derives from the Declaration of Arbroath and can be seen as an indigenous expression of the international concept of 'peaceful enjoyment'.

The requirement for powers of compulsory purchase through the state has long been well established.[3] They are based on the underlying justification "that the loss of private land is offset by the gain to the wider community to which those individuals belong".[4] The fact that this justification has also been used by proponents of comprehensive land nationalisation has always made compulsory purchase a particularly sensitive political issue. Those opposed to compulsory purchase have often used terms such as 'appropriation' in a prejudicial way to try and enhance a sense of compulsory purchase as an illegitimate act.

Compulsory purchase is an act of last resort, used if land can not be acquired on the open market or by an agreed sale. The sense of 'last resort' does not detract from the extremely practical importance of compulsory purchase as a positive tool in a modern (post-) industrial society (for example, acquiring properties to enable major urban redevelopment projects). To this end, compulsory purchase has become increasingly used for a widening range of purposes by governments of all political persuasions. While the use has mainly been in an urban context, there is no distinction in the scope of compulsory purchase powers to prevent them being similarly used in rural areas.

The value of compulsory purchase to society has led during the 20th century to continuing reforms towards a "simpler, more uniform, less costly and more expeditious system for the compulsory purchase of land".[5] The introduction of a reformed system of land tenure in Scotland would provide a particular opportunity to maintain that process with further refinements that reflect an appropriate balance between public and private interests. As part of this, the commitment to compensation could be formalised as a right in legislation. This long-standing commitment is reflected in the use of the label 'purchase' with its implication of payment. However, at present, compensation is only a matter of judicial presumption. The general rule is that compensation will be payable unless it is specifically precluded by legislation in particular circumstances. The original *raison d'être* for the Lands Tribunal for Scotland was to provide systematic arrangements for determining the value of compensation in individual situations.

Consolidating and amending legislation for the operation of compulsory purchase in Scotland could also formalise and rationalise a number of other existing provisions to safeguard private interests (for example, the scope for people to object and their rights as objectors, and the restrictions ensuring that compulsory purchase can only be used where its purpose has been adequately specified). In addition, for example, the fate of compulsorily acquired land that is no longer required for its original purpose could be clarified, including setting a time limit to any continuing interest of the former private owner.

At the same time, there is a need to define compulsory purchase in ways fully adapted to contemporary circumstances. While these powers have traditionally been associated with government agencies and local authorities, the boundaries between public and private sectors are now more indistinct. Clarification is therefore required of the types of bodies in which the powers of compulsory purchase can be reasonably vested. This is also linked to delimiting powers that are akin to compulsory purchase but fall short of it. These powers are labelled compulsory rights. They cover the authority, for example, to lay cables and other utilities across private land.

More generally still, there is the need to establish a clear distinction between compulsory purchase and regulation, together with associated rules governing when compensation is or is not due.[6] Land ownership is now more properly seen in terms of the ownership of rights over land, rather than more absolute notions of the ownership of the land itself. Thus, legislation to regulate the use of land that extinguishes a particular right over land may amount to the appropriation of that right by the state and thus be a matter for compensation.[7] The interpretation of this issue has become central to the balance of public and private interests in land tenure (see below).

Voluntary Principle

Different countries vary in the extent to which they use land tenure and its associated legal arrangements to regulate the ownership and use of land in the public interest. In Britain, the level of this statutory regulation is low compared to most European countries.[8] This British position reflects a reliance on voluntary action and is often described as being based on the voluntary principle. There is no established definition of this principle despite the widespread references to it by government and others. It can, however, be seen as a broad principle of public policy that seeks to achieve as much as possible without legislation and so fulfil policy aims through persuasion (education), incentives (rewards) and collaboration (co-operation) rather than legal compulsion.

In these terms, the voluntary principle might be considered generally uncontroversial. However, recent Conservative governments were criticised by some for using the voluntary principle as an excuse for not acting decisively on particular land use issues.[9] With deer management in the Highlands, for example, many have argued that persuasion has failed to ensure that land owners adequately control the high numbers of red deer and that therefore compulsory powers should be used.

The voluntary principle starts from the universal aim of supporting individual freedom and is closely related to the principle of subsidiarity – that decision making should be allowed to take place as close as possible to the action, while still producing results compatible with the public interest. The voluntary principle thus rests on the proposition that allowing persons to act of their own free will (i.e. voluntarily) gives better long term results by promoting personal motivation and allowing the flexibility for decisions to be adapted to particular circumstances. While the voluntary principle is based on the concept of two parties (the actor and a higher authority), it operates between many different players/partners at many different levels in all spheres of public policy.

The voluntary principle can be seen as aiming to achieve fine-tuning in the delivery of public policy below the level of legislation. It should come after non-negotiable and enforceable minimum standards have been set. New legislation should not necessarily be seen as an erosion of the voluntary principle, but as a redefinition of the framework beyond which the voluntary principle operates. Land use activities continue to change (for example, through innovation and new technologies) and public perceptions evolve (for example, over acceptable standards of land management) and with them the scope for the voluntary principle.

The extent of reliance on the voluntary principle is a matter which goes beyond land tenure issues and into wider philosophies of government. To aim at as little legislation as possible may seem straightforward, but a more negative perspective on the relative importance of the voluntary principle in Britain is that it is a product of very centralised government. Reliance on the voluntary principle becomes a requirement where limited legislative opportunities mean that detailed legislation would become significantly out of date and potentially obstructive before the next chance to revise it. The Parliament of, for example, a federal state such as Bavaria (which is approximately the size of Scotland), is able to leave less to chance by enacting legislation on issues that can currently only be covered by broad policy statements in Britain.

The new Scottish Parliament can be expected to have a commitment to the voluntary principle, but it will be able to legislate to a new level of detail on land ownership and use. This will enable the boundaries for where the voluntary principle begins and ends (the minimum acceptable standards required) to be clearly and consistently defined in a modernised and reformed system of land tenure.

Statutory Limitations

It is basic to democratic government, and thus a fundamental principle of land ownership, that the rights associated with land ownership always yield to the public interest.[10] This is an ongoing process under the influence of parliamentary legislation and affects both the rights of property that come with land ownership and how those rights can be exercised. In this web of inter-acting laws, there are no distinct boundaries between the laws of land tenure and administrative laws that affect the use of land.[11]

The modern growth of this framework of statutory regulation around land ownership started with public health and safety laws in the 19th century and has continued through this century with other socio-economic concerns and the rapid expansion over recent decades in environmental legislation.[12]

Every year, new legislation on a wide range of issues continues to affect land ownership directly or indirectly and this requires an ongoing balance to be struck between private and public interests. A crucial frontier in this is the distinction between the regulation and the removal of property rights. In particular, this involves defining situations when compensation is, or is not, considered due. Debate over this boundary is associated with the concept of 'takings', an American term which derives from the US Constitution's 5th Amendment: "private property . . . (shall not) . . . be taken for public use without just compensation".[13] Thus a regulation that 'goes too far' becomes a 'taking'.

The changing view of property has opened up the scope of what now might be considered a taking. Property has become recognised not as objects, but rights which attach to physical objects and thus, the removal of individual or particular rights by regulation can be construed to be a taking. Thus, it has become less clear where the boundary is between a regulation and a taking. If a reasonable balance is not struck, there is the danger that regulation in the public interest is reduced, as government action is inhibited by concerns about compensation expenditure.

The issue of takings is more extreme in the USA than Britain. This results from a combination of legal and cultural factors, both reflected in the USA's land tenure system. US law came from English law, and the laws of land tenure were shaped by the ambition of Thomas Jefferson and others, drawing on Locke's views on property, to escape the vestiges of feudalism in the English system at that time.[14] This led to a strongly entrenched position on the absolute dominion of private owners over their land, reflected in the homestead legislation of the 19th century. This has produced ongoing conflict over the issue of takings, which has intensified over recent decades under the increase in environmental regulation required by society. Authoritative calls have been made in the USA for the provisions over takings to be radically reformed to reduce the influence of landed interests.[15]

The general difference between the American and British positions on this issue have been recognised, including the dangers of American influence,[16] but little attention has been paid yet to the differences between English and Scots law. The legal interests of private owner-ship against the public interest may be weaker in England than the USA, but they are significantly stronger than in Scotland. In England, the tradition of the pre-conquest Saxon freemen, used by Jefferson in the US system, has in fact always survived and underpinned strong private interests, allowing virtually no identity for the Crown in land tenure. The English equivalent to the US 'homestead' mentality is the notion of the Englishman in his castle.

By contrast, in Scotland, the survival of the Paramount Superior and shared property interests in any piece of land has created a situation that underpins a different legal attitude to private interests. This is a tradition of a stronger public interest stake in the owner-ship of land than in either the USA or England. An appropriate Scottish term for a taking which reflects this might be, after Erskine, a 'limitation' (see page 61).

The general rule in Britain is that no compensation is due for regulation and this needs to be maintained, subject to provision for cases of transitional hardship under new regulations. The reform of land tenure in Scotland provides the opportunity to draw a clear line through the increasing maze of property rights and rights of use and set a strict boundary for what might be considered a taking or statutory limitation. An appropriate divide should both recognise the legitimate rights of private ownership and ensure full opportunity to pursue the public interest effectively.

Reform would be eased by a general recognition that regulations are not simply burdens on private interests. Fair regulations should be construed as imposing responsibilities on private interests. For an extreme example, the prohibition of slavery (in which Scotland was a medieval pioneer!) can not rightly be seen as simply a burden on private interests. Similarly, meeting certain public standards in the ownership and management of land, might be seen as a matter of fulfilling responsibilities. A reformed system of tenure in Scotland provides a crucial opportunity to define clearly in contemporary terms the rights and responsibilities of private ownership in relationship to the public interest.

Land Tribunal

A land tenure system, as the legal framework governing the ownership and use of land, inevitably gives rise to legal disputes, or at least issues of interpretation. While such matters can be dealt with through conventional courts, it has long been recognised in Scotland that there are practical advantages in having a specialised court or tribunal as the first port of call for particular land tenure matters.

Scotland already has two such bodies: the Scottish Land Court and the Lands Tribunal for Scotland. They have distinct functions but are closely related, as reflected in their shared address in Edinburgh and the fact that the Chairman of the Court is also President of the Tribunal.

The Scottish Land Court is a fairly distinctive Scottish institution, with very few countries in the world having an equivalent body.[17] It was constituted in 1912 under the Small Landholders (Scotland) Act 1911. It took over the legal functions of the original Crofters Commission established in 1886, and had similar responsibilities for landholdings over the whole of Scotland. Under legislation in 1931, its jurisdiction was expanded to a wide range of matters relating to farms of all kinds in Scotland. This was further extended by the Agricultural Holdings (Scotland) Act 1949, although the Crofters (Scotland) Act 1955 transferred many of the Land Court's responsibilities in the Crofting Counties to the new Crofters Commission.

The scope to establish Lands Tribunals in England (Wales), Northern Ireland and Scotland derived from the Lands Tribunal Act 1949 and was originally related to the issue of valuations in compulsory purchase cases. The Lands Tribunal for Scotland, however, was not established until 1971, essentially in response to the Conveyancing and Feudal Reform (Scotland) Act 1970. In addition to compulsory purchase issues, this gave the Tribunal responsibilities in relation to matters such as feudal conditions and feu duties. Also, since its inception, an ever-expanding list of legislation has brought an increasingly diverse and comprehensive range of matters relating to land within its sphere.[18]

The Land Court and Tribunal are part of the Scottish Courts Administration and fully integrated into the Scottish court system. The Tribunal, for example, follows the procedures of the Court of Session and Sheriff Courts where matters are not covered by its own rules, while the Chairman of the Land Court has the equivalent rank to a Court of Session judge. Rights of appeal are linked to Scotland's other courts and those courts must not intrude on the judgements or orders of the Land Court or Tribunal.

Both the Land Court and Tribunal have considerable flexibility in practice and procedure to fit circumstances. The rules governing the Tribunal incorporate a statement to that effect, while the Land Court, for example, has the power to appoint specialists to sit with it, to delegate authority and to hold its sessions anywhere it chooses. The scope of the Land Court to 'go on the road' and aspects such as its compulsory incorporation of a Gaelic speaker have also made it particularly adaptable.

With the replacement of feudal tenure and other potential changes affecting the existing roles of the Tribunal and Land Court (for example, changes to agricultural and crofting legislation), there is considerable opportunity to integrate these two bodies and give them a more comprehensive role on land tenure matters within a reformed system of land tenure. Many issues associated with disputes over administrative law could also be brought within their remit (for example, in relation to Forestry Authority Felling Licences or Deer Commission compulsory control schemes). In wider terms still, the Tribunal and Land Court could form the basis of a new Lands Commission for Scotland.

Conclusions from Section 2

Chapter 4 *The Involvement of the Crown*

- Scotland has continued to be a sovereign nation since the Union of Parliaments in 1707 and Scotland's separate system of land tenure is based on and derived from those sovereign rights.
- The special roles of the Crown in the legal jurisdictions north and south of the border also continued after the Union and the Crown's position in Scotland's system of land tenure is based on its distinct constitutional identity in Scotland.
- Sovereignty in Scotland is founded in constitutional law on the sovereignty of the people and, as popularly expressed over the centuries, the Crown is the representative of the Community of the Realm.

Chapter 5 *The Underlying Framework*

- In Scotland's system of land tenure, under the Crown's sovereign rights, parts of the territory of Scotland and certain rights over all the territory are held inalienably in trust for the people of Scotland in the Crown's name.
- While the Crown's rights are all subject to the will of Parliament, the Crown can be considered as a permanent representation of the public interest and Parliament as the contemporary expression of that public interest at any point in time.
- The ownership of land in Scotland is essentially defined as holding a valid title to that land and there is now the opportunity to put in place both a new, unified form of tenure and a comprehensive system of registration of titles to land.

Chapter 6 *Public and Private Interests*

- The rights of land owners in Scotland could be improved by many measures ranging from the abolition of feudal tenure to the adoption in UK law of the European Convention on Human Rights.

- A balance has to be struck through Parliament between securing the peaceful enjoyment of their land by owners and statutory regulation that is deemed necessary to safeguard the public interest.
- The conditional nature of feudal tenure is a legacy that should enable a new system of land tenure in Scotland to more readily strike an appropriate balance between public and private interests, than the more absolute notions of ownership in most other countries.

SECTION THREE
Public Rights in Land

CHAPTER SEVEN

Scotland's Sovereign Lands

Territory

The 'land' covered by Scotland's land tenure system coincides, by definition, with the territory of Scotland. The outer boundaries of this territory are legally defined. They delimit the jurisdiction of Scots law deriving from sovereign authority and identify where that jurisdiction borders either with adjoining sovereign territories or shared international territory (often referred to as the 'global commons').

However, these boundaries are not just lines on a map. They have to be considered in both horizontal and vertical dimensions, with the overall extent of Scotland's territory being a volume rather than a simple surface area. The sovereign territory of Scotland is, as with that of other sovereign nations, considered to extend above and below its surface boundaries down to the centre of the earth and up to the outer limits of the atmosphere. In these broadest terms, the territory of Scotland is a 'cone', reaching from the centre of the Earth some 6356 kilometres (3950 miles) below Scotland's surface and spreading up through the various atmospheric layers above it: from the Troposphere, which goes up approximately 11 kilometres (36,000 feet) above sea level and represents 80% of the total mass of the atmosphere, to the start of the Exosphere at around 650 kilometres (400 miles).

Scotland's surface boundaries have evolved over the centuries with the additions of the Western and Northern Isles in the 13th and 15th centuries respectively, and adjustments in the details of the land boundary with England continuing over subsequent centuries. That land boundary was essentially settled in the 19th century, although special provisions continue to be made to clarify the respective administrative responsibilities for rivers that form part of the boundary.[1] The marine area covered has also changed. The outer boundary of Scotland's territorial waters has been expanded relatively recently to 12 nautical miles and additional rights are also now claimed beyond that (see Chapter 9).

Scotland's total surface area is 177,511 square kilometres, made up of land and inland water covering 78,789 square kilometres and an estimated seabed area of 98,722 square kilometres. The scale of this surface area can be set in a global context to illustrate the share of the Earth within the sphere of Scotland's system of land tenure. There are a number of variables in the global statistics available (for example, the inclusion or exclusion of permanent ice), but the Earth's total surface area is approximately 510,069,120 square kilometres (of which Scotland's share is 0.03%), made up of 148,328,100 square kilometres of land and inland water (Scotland's share is 0.05%) and a marine area of 361,741,020 square kilometres (Scotland's share is 0.03%).

Scotland's land and inland water therefore accounts for approximately 1/2000th of the Earth's land and inland area. Scotland's sovereign land tenure system is also set in context by the fact that jurisdiction over this global land area is divided up between nearly 200 such sovereign systems (see below).

Realm

Constitutionally, the ultimate ownership of the territory of Scotland as a sovereign nation is vested in the Crown. The territory is thus synonymous with the *Realm of Scotland*, while the Crown itself represents the Community of the Realm (see Chapter 4). This ultimate ownership encompasses the whole territory and all its natural assets. It is the starting point of land tenure in Scotland and the authority from which all other rights of ownership, occupancy and use of the territory derive. The Crown holds the territory on behalf of the Community of the Realm and all other rights are then held under and from the Crown.

A fundamental split in Scotland's system of land tenure is between the rights over the territory retained by the Crown and those that are granted out to others. Under the present system, the Crown retains complete ownership of specified parts of the territory and particular rights over all of it. The reform of land tenure in Scotland would provide the opportunity to clarify and refine the extent and nature of both of these.

The need for this arises from several different causes. The abolition of feudalism will, by definition, remove the Crown's position as Paramount Superior and a restatement will be required to consolidate the Crown's role in land tenure under its identity as Sovereign. This should include achieving the same status for the Crown throughout the Realm by resolving the ambiguities that exist between the Northern Isles and the rest of Scotland in terms of which of the Crown's rights are rights of sovereignty and which derive from its feudal status as Paramount Superior. This need not end the scope for local distinctiveness in the land tenure arrangements in the Northern Isles.

A wider requirement is to remove the doubts and confusions that have built up over the nature of some of the actual rights the Crown either retains or grants out. Several factors have given rise to these uncertainties, including the generally ancient nature of the Scots system and the relative lack of attention given to it over recent centuries in the Westminster Parliament.

The modern position of the Crown in Scotland essentially stems from the institutional writers of the 17th and 18th centuries, such as Stair. In the period since, changes have mainly been made by the Scottish courts evolving the law through precedent. This process means that some aspects of the Crown's rights have not been dealt with for a long time. A new statement of the law would allow ambiguities to be resolved and various archaic rights to be tidied away once and for all (for example, the concept that some species, such as some whales, are 'Royal animals' – see Chapter 9).

This modernisation would also allow some particular rights to be strengthened to reflect contemporary circumstances. Some instances might be relatively minor adjustments, for example, that the public right of navigation in some rivers should incorporate a right of recreational swimming rather than just narrowly defined rights of passage.[2] With others, the consolidation of a number of changes might amount to a more profound fresh interpretation (for example, establishing clearly the legal basis of the public interest in the welfare of wild animals – see Chapter 9).

These types of changes have to be seen in the context of the erosion during the 18th and 19th centuries of the public interest in land as represented by the Crown. During these centuries, there was a strong tendency to promote private rather than public rights. The way particular Court of Session judges could contribute to this is illustrated by some of Lord Inglis's decisions. He decided, for example, in an 1870s case, that certain public rights in rivers derived through the Crown should only exist where the rivers are tidal – instead of the former position where these rights also extended as far as rivers were navigable. He was also the judge who made the decision that first allowed land owners to start leasing out their sporting rights, when these right had previously been considered a natural incident of land and not capable of being separated into a lease (see Chapter 14).

This century, the potential significance to the public interest of Crown rights in Scotland's land has continued to diminish. This has been through neglect of the distinctive nature of the Crown in Scotland during this century's major growth in both UK statute law and the role of the state. The Crown is superficially similar north and south of the border. In both cases, the ultimate ownership of territory is still vested in the Crown and the Crown is, of course, represented in each case by the same monarch. The key difference is sovereignty, but Westminster follows the English position on the sovereignty of Parliament for UK legislation and under this, the Crown's significance is minimised. This influence is not working directly through Scots land law, which is still the subject of separate legislation, but through the general convergence of English and Scots law and the growth of areas of UK legislation that impact on Scots land law (for example, the wide category of legislation now labelled environmental law).

In this context, the doctrine of the sovereignty of Parliament essentially allows for just one expression of public interest – Parliament operating through the state. Distinctions between Crown property and state property are diminished, with further confusion arising from the way that state property is classified as Crown property because it is held by *Her Majesty's* government.

In Scotland, due to the sovereignty of the people, there are two principal levels of public interest. There is both the Community of the Realm (nation) and Parliament (state). Parliament gives contemporary and practical expression to the underlying principles of public interest represented by the concept of the Community of the Realm. These two levels should be clearly recognised both with respect to the Crown's rights retained in all land and in the distinction between Crown property and state property. The difference between these latter two is that between, for example, the ownership of Scotland's territorial seas, held inalienably in trust for the people of Scotland by the Crown, and land for Forest Enterprise plantations acquired (and disposed of) by the government representing the state. The state, while it can acquire land by means not available to other owners, is just another land owner holding property through a title derived from the Crown.

A new Parliament in Scotland provides the opportunity for a new statement of Scotland's land laws to clarify and redefine the Crown's rights and interests in land, redetermining where necessary its relationship with state and privately owned land. The Crown's significance in land tenure in Scotland has become increasingly marginalised during the last 100 years, even in its treatment in Scots law books. These tend to continue the 19th century trend towards seeing the Crown's interests in all land as a burden on private ownership, rather than a positive statement in the public interest.

Beyond the Realm

There is an international dimension to Scotland's system of land tenure that derives from Scotland's status as a distinct sovereign territory. That sovereignty confers various rights and responsibilities under international law that extend beyond the territorial boundaries of Scotland.

The world's surface can be divided into the sovereign territories of states and the areas in between. These latter areas are the high seas – international waters shared in common by all sovereign states. The exception to this pattern is Antarctica, the Earth's only significant land mass outwith sovereign territory. The Antarctic is subject to claims of sovereignty by several countries, including the UK. However, under the Antarctic Treaty, these claims are set aside and the signatories work together to govern the continent.

The extent of both sovereign territories and the high seas incorporates the ground beneath them and the air space above. An additional dimension is outer space which, like the high seas, is shared in common under international law by all sovereign states. A substantial body of international space law has developed although, it might be noted, there has never been agreement on how to define the boundary between air space and outer space.

International law deals with the rights and duties of sovereign states both between each other and with respect to the high seas or global commons. The law is based on sovereignty as a two-fold concept. Firstly, it refers to internal competence to exercise authority within territorial boundaries. Secondly, sovereignty confers equality of status under international law. The actual laws involved are defined by United Nations General Assembly Resolutions, multilateral conventions, treaties and the decisions of the international courts.

There are several issues in this situation that could be addressed as part of the reform of Scotland's system of land tenure. One of these issues is the need to consolidate and refine the major changes under international law in recent decades which have expanded Scotland's territory further out to sea. These changes are described below (see Chapter 9), but determining the outer boundary of Scotland's sovereign territory is not a matter of a straightforward line on the map and raises two other closely related issues. Firstly, the need to clarify the relationship between the Crown and the state in UK law in the complex pattern of sovereign rights now claimed under international law between the shore and the high seas. Secondly, leading on from this, the need to clarify the status of Scotland's sovereign territory in international law.

While the first issue revolves around the distinct identity of the Crown in Scotland, the second relates to Scotland's exceptional position as a sovereign nation without statehood. The relevant international law is generally expressed in terms of sovereign states. However, particularly as a result of the era of decolonisation, international law allows for countries with even lesser status than Scotland, for example, Namibia when it was still a dependency of South Africa.

While Scotland meets the requirement of sovereign territory, the first basic criterion of a state, it also has other necessary attributes such as legal personality and a high degree of internal competence.

The establishment of the Scottish Parliament will improve the situation further, as would the reassertion in a UK context of the Crown's distinct identity in Scotland. Significantly, it is the Crown that is constitutionally responsible for signing treaties as part of its prerogative. More specifically, if it appeared appropriate, this would allow for particular international conventions to be ratified and adopted for Scottish waters alone and not the UK waters as a whole. The adoption would be by incorporation directly into Scots law rather than UK law. This need not compromise the Treaties of Union and a parallel option could exist for England and Wales.

All Scotland's territorial boundaries are, of course, marine with the exception of the short land frontier with England. A relatively limited proportion of the marine boundaries are with other UK jurisdictions and the advent of the off-shore oil and gas industry has been one factor clarifying and reinforcing the distinctiveness of these jurisdictions. Otherwise, the great majority of Scotland's boundary is international, either with individual neighbouring foreign jurisdictions (Norway and Eire, with the marine boundary with Eire redefined in 1987) or with the high seas. This extensive international frontier gives Scotland a particularly strong interest in marine issues and there are opportunities to give that interest more tangible expression. The rights that now extend beyond the territorial sea, including rights to exploit and manage the marine environment (see Chapter 9), are rights of a proprietorial character dependent on Scotland's sovereignty and can be regarded as *parts and pertinents* within its land tenure system.

CHAPTER EIGHT

The Crown Estate

The Regalia

Scotland's territory is traditionally identified as the *kingdom* of Scotland. Within the kingdom, the 'attributes of kingly power' held by the Crown are known as the *regality*. The Crown's rights of a proprietorial character in and over the territory are technically referred to as the *regalia*. The regalia are usually classified into the *regalia majora* and *regalia minora*.

The regalia majora are the rights held inalienably by the Crown in trust for the people of Scotland. They include the rights over specific parts of the territory retained by the Crown (for example, territorial seas) and the rights retained by the Crown in the parts of the territory granted out into ownership (for example, 'treasure trove' – the right to any treasure found within Scotland). The regalia minora are other rights held by the Crown which can be granted out into ownership. These rights cover both particular areas (for example, the foreshore) and specific activities (for example, salmon fishing rights).

The main part of Scotland's surface area that is held in trust for the people of Scotland is the surrounding sea. Scotland is enclosed by sea, except for the short land boundary with England, and in fact Scotland's marine territory is more extensive than Scotland's land and inland water area (see Chapter 7). This marine environment and its natural resources have been and continue to be of major economic importance. There are, of course, many problems associated with the management and use of Scotland's marine environment, such as overfishing.

The appropriation of Scotland's marine environment and its main component resources into conventional state and private ownership, while presenting some practical difficulties, would not be impossible. Dividing the sea up into different properties would have appeared much more difficult in previous centuries with their more limited technology. However, as spelt out by Stair in his pioneering 17th century statement of the laws of Scotland, holding the marine environment as a shared asset for the benefit of the people of Scotland was not just a consequence of practical difficulties. It was a positive choice that this important resource should be held in common for the whole population.

The Crown's 'in trust ownership' of the marine environment is conceived as extending both down to the centre of the Earth (over 6000 kilometres) and up to the upper limit of the atmosphere (over 600 kilometres). It might be considered that, in either direction, well before these distances are being approached, the idea of national sovereignty has become fairly notional. Both the Earth's core and the upper atmosphere are more appropriately seen as part of the global commons shared between nations.

It is clearer still that even within relatively short distances above or below Scotland's land surface (say, 10 kilometres), there is little meaning to the idea of individual private property. However, the current system of land ownership persists in the view that land granted out by the Crown into ownership is still *a coelo usque ad centrum* (i.e. to the height of the Heavens and the centre of the Earth). This rule comes from times when knowledge of what was implied was very limited compared to the present day. More meaningful and realistic boundaries could now be set to ownership above and below the land surface (see Chapter 9). Beyond these limits, all interests would be held, as with the territorial seas, by the Crown in trust for the people of Scotland. This reform would essentially just give practical effect in legal terms to what might already be considered legitimate reality.

This adjustment would consolidate a fundamental perspective that sets ownership of the actual land surface in context: it is enclosed – up in the air, under the ground and out to sea – by territory held by the Crown in trust for the people of Scotland.

With regard to the land itself (including freshwater), only a limited extent of this surface area is held directly in trust by the Crown. The nature and extent of these areas does need to be reviewed and this could lead to both losses and gains, as described in the next chapter. However, in general terms, there is relatively little pretext for the land itself to be retained directly by the Crown.

With the land surface, the basic public interest is entrenched through the rights retained by the Crown over all land in ownership (and which are described in Chapter 10). These Crown rights are essentially the terms and conditions under which land is granted out into ownership: they define ownership as a public interest mechanism in which everything is underpinned by a public interest commitment. Within the logic of even the current system, these retained rights are a positive public interest statement. They are not, as some legal texts appear to suggest, simply burdens and inconveniences on the freedom of action of owners.

Reforming land tenure would provide an opportunity to clarify and refine at a technical level the details of the regalia, including how they are interpreted and implemented. This would create a fresh climate of awareness about the fundamental position of the rights held by the Crown in trust for the public and underpin a proper balance between public and private interests in the management of Scotland's natural resources.

Regime

The rights and interests in land held by the Crown in trust for the public are diverse and extensive. While they can be classified in various ways, four broad categories of rights and interests have been identified here:

(i)   those held internationally relative to other jurisdictions and the global commons;

(ii) those held inalienably over parts of the territory not granted out into ownership;

(iii) those still held inalienably over all land granted into ownership;

(iv) those held within the territory that may or may not be granted out.

There is, of course, nothing absolute about any of these rights and interests. It is within Parliament's power to alter all or any of them, whether in their existence or operation. While some of the rights are described as inalienable, meaning that their ownership can not be transferred, this can be overturned by legislation. Inalienability is simply a statement of principle given effect in law. It is based on the philosophical premise, first fully articulated by Stair over 300 years ago, that there are certain rights and interests in the territory of Scotland that should be held for ever for the common good of the whole population of Scotland. The special importance of these rights is entrenched by making them inalienable.

Society's views over what exactly should be held inalienably, and the interpretation of this into law, evolves over time. Parliament could legislate for certain state-owned lands to be held inalienably (for example, as with National Parks in the USA). However, at present, the status of inalienability continues to represent a key marker between Crown property and state property. Having the open sea inalienable, for example, means it can not readily be 'privatised' and that any loop-hole that might allow areas of open sea to be appropriated into private ownership, should be closed off as a matter of policy. While inalienability is not a status accorded to state land, it is attributed to certain properties held by the National Trust for Scotland. This unique provision in Scots law dates from the 1930s and might now be considered due for review (see Chapter 9). Under the provision, the National Trust for Scotland Council can decide that a property will be held inalienably and so prevent their successors from disposing of that property except in exceptional circumstances.

More generally, the reform of land tenure provides the opportunity to develop a modern public interest statement of Crown rights and interests. The conversion of this into law would reduce the current reliance on common law interpretations by replacing them with statutory representations. This has happened from time to time in relation to particular rights (for example, the conversion of the Crown's authority to make grants to establish ports and harbours into statutory provisions during the early 19th century), but a systematic approach could now be taken. This greater reliance on statutes would result in some elements becoming more explicitly subject to state control and management. However, constitutionally and in the public interest, this rationalisation should not lead to simple *nationalisation* (state ownership) of what are held to be the core inalienable Crown rights and interests.

The Crown/state distinction could be expressed in a new statement of the differences between *res communis* and *res publica*. The use of these traditional labels has become inconsistent since Stair and others in that same era. As collectively owned things, they can be contrasted with *res privatus*. The maintenance of the necessary distinctions between Crown and State in this context requires some degree of representation and administration for Crown rights and interests that is separate in part from the government of the day. Some of these rights and interests are more or less statements of principle (notably category iii above) to which Parliament gives effect through legislation, state agencies and other means. Other existing Crown rights and interests require more direct physical administration (for example, areas of land in category ii above). Such areas may be managed day-to-day by a state agency or other body, but the management may need to have a different emphasis from that on other properties managed by any such agency on the basis that only 'special areas' should continue to be held by the Crown. This specialness might result from the area's special historic or constitutional significance, with Edinburgh Castle as perhaps the most conspicuous example.

The Crown's rights and interests in land have traditionally been known as the Crown Estate and are currently represented and administered by the Crown Estate Commission (CEC). Any review of these Crown rights and interests (as proposed here) should also review this regime.

Commission

The Crown Estate Commission (CEC) was established earlier this century as the successor to previous bodies that have managed the Crown Estate since 1760, when that Estate was originally distanced from Royal control and any surplus annual income started to be surrendered to Parliament in exchange for the Civil List. The CEC is currently constituted under the Crown Estate Act 1961 and operates under the terms of that Act and subsidiary legislation. The CEC has a UK remit and is responsible for what the CEC describes as the hereditary possessions of the Sovereign 'in right of the Crown' (their inverted commas).[1] The Crown Estate Commissioners are appointed by and report to the Sovereign and to Parliament. Under the 1961 Act, the general duty of the

Commissioners for the Crown Estate is "to maintain and enhance its value and the return obtained from it, but with due regard to the requirements of good management". The Act gives the Commissioners an extraordinary degree of immunity from being questioned about their activities.[2]

While some might criticise the land use and administrative standards of the CEC, the issue here is the whole ethos and legal framework that directs the CEC's operation. The modernisation of Scotland's system of land tenure should include consideration of the appropriateness of the CEC as an administrative arrangement for managing the Crown Estate in Scotland.

At present, the CEC and its management might be characterised as little different from a conventional investment and estate management company (see Chapter 9). The CEC's narrow interpretation of its statutory responsibility for the value of the Crown Estate is exemplified by the very extensive and active involvement of the CEC in buying and selling urban properties as part of its investment portfolio. There are close and telling parallels between the CEC's involvements with the urban property investment market and those of the Duchy of Cornwall – the substantial estate spread over two dozen English counties, incorporating specific rights usually held by the Crown (for example, extensive lengths of foreshore) and first established in the 14th century to provide an income for the heir to the throne of England. Historically, while the Duchy supported the heir, the Crown Estate supported the Sovereign. The Duchy still pays money in trust for the heir/Duke of Cornwall, while the Crown Estate pays money to the treasury for the Civil List. However, there remain very close links in England between the CEC and the Duchy, including the fact that several of the Duchy Trustees serve as Crown Estate Commissioners.

These links reflect a wider case for greater distance to be put between the Crown Estate and the monarch. This includes the need to make the appointment and performance of Commissioners more democratically accountable and to abolish the apparent option for monarchs at accession to adopt Crown Estate revenues in preference to the Civil List. However, the parallels between the CEC and Duchy also reflect the essentially English origin and character of the CEC. Scotland did have its own equivalent to the Duchy – the Principality of Scotland, also established from the 14th century and for similar reasons as the Duchy (see Chapter 4). However, in contrast to the vast territory of the Duchy, the Principality only survives as remnant feudal superiorities which are scheduled to be abolished with feudal tenure in Scotland. There is a similar contrast between the scale of the interests of the CEC in England and Scotland, with Scotland only accounting for 4% of the total capital value of the Crown Estate and 6% of the gross revenue.[3]

The management approach adopted by the CEC, particularly since the 1970s with the commercial leasing of rights in the marine environment (for example, fish cages and mooring rights), can also be viewed as deriving from its English base. This is underpinned by the fact that the legal test cases that have allowed this approach to be developed are seen as having followed English precedent.[4] This, in turn, might be traced back to the fact that the CEC was constituted in 1961 as a UK body, when it might have been expected on legal authority that a distinct arrangement would have been put in place for Scotland.

The Crown's rights and interests in Scotland's land, encompassing "the hereditary possessions of the Sovereign in right of the Crown", attach to the distinct identity of the Crown in Scotland. The CEC can only legitimately derive its mandate in Scotland from that distinctiveness and this should be reflected in the nature of the CEC in Scotland. The CEC in Scotland should not only operate under Scots land law, but should also be constituted within it. One reflection of the situation is that the resources for which the CEC has responsibility in Scotland, for example the foreshore, are defined and governed by Scots law.

The reform of Scotland's system of land tenure should provide an opportunity to review the position of the CEC in Scotland and establish new administrative arrangements for the Crown Estate in Scotland. This could allow changes to a democratically accountable system and a move away from the standard landlord approach of the CEC, albeit over resources not usually in the private sector, to an approach that reflects the status of the Crown Estate lands and resources as common property resources to be managed meaningfully for the benefit of the people of Scotland.

The Secretary of State for Scotland currently has a power of direction over the CEC in Scotland under the 1961 Crown Estate Act and it might be anticipated that, in line with such other powers of direction over public bodies, this power will be transferred to the Scottish Parliament. The draft devolution legislation, however, specifically identifies the CEC as a reserved matter. Therefore it will not be possible as things stand for the Scottish Parliament to establish a separate body for Scotland, as it will be able to for other public sector bodies with GB or UK remits that do not deal with reserved matters (for example, the Forestry Commission).[5] However, the CEC is only an administrative arrangement, not a constitutional matter, and the basis for the Scottish Parliament having the authority to replace the CEC in Scotland has been set out above. A replacement Scottish body for the CEC could be appointed by and report to the Scottish Parliament. Additionally, although this involves wider issues, any surplus income from the Crown Estate in Scotland might be surrendered to the Scottish Parliament.

In considering the future management of the Crown Estate, it might be doubted whether a successor organisation to the CEC is required, even if it was constituted within Scotland's law. Provision could be made for all or most of the CEC's resource management responsibilities to be delegated to government bodies, local authorities and other more local democratic bodies. The Shetland Isles, where the Crown Estate holds limited rights, already provide examples of local authority control. Under such delegation of the responsibilities currently undertaken by the CEC, the land and natural resources involved would still be held inalienably in trust for the people of Scotland. They would thus not be 'owned' by the government body or local authority managing it. Delegation of the management would not amount to nationalisation and with it, the scope for subsequent alienation into private ownership.

The transfer of the CEC's responsibilities to democratically accountable bodies in Scotland need not preclude the possibility of a small commission which would have an overview of the land and natural resources held in trust by the Crown, as well as representing the Crown's rights and interests generally in land. Commissioners in any such body might be appointed only by Parliament and seen as similar to Privy Councillors in their general standing and regard in society. It might be noted that the office of Privy Councillor in Scotland has not existed since the Scottish Privy Council was abolished in 1708.

CHAPTER NINE

Natural Assets Held by the Public

Marine Environment

Scotland is largely surrounded by sea. Indeed, the natural wealth and resources of Scotland's marine environment are one of the country's most basic assets.

This marine territory stretches from the upper tidal reaches of rivers and the foreshore, out across the surrounding seas. Its outer boundaries are formed, in part, by neighbouring jurisdictions, and over an extensive frontier, by the high seas. The extent of the marine territory between these inner and outer boundaries has increased very substantially over recent decades, as the UK, in common with most sovereign states, has laid claim since the Second World War to sovereign rights much further out to sea than previously.

This expansion has involved three elements. Firstly, the distance to the edge of territorial waters has been pushed out from three to twelve nautical miles. Secondly, at the same time, a more generous interpretation has been used of where the measurement starts from around the coast (see below). Thirdly, sovereign rights are also now claimed over the sea and sea-bed for a further 200 miles beyond the territorial boundary.

The distribution of rights and interests in this marine environment follows the different zones involved, namely, the foreshore, tidal rivers and other internal waters, the territorial seas to the three and twelve mile limits, and, beyond them, exclusive fishery and economic zones and the continental shelf, and then the high seas. These zones run as a transect of interests out from the land.

The foreshore in Scotland (but not the rest of the UK) is between the Low and High Water Marks of ordinary spring tides, while the extent of tidal rivers is determined by the movement of salt water, not by any influence the tide may have on the level of flow further upstream. The internal waters of Scotland are those areas of sea water between the foreshore and the base lines used to measure out to the twelve mile territorial limit. The international rules adopted by the UK in 1987 for setting base lines allow these lines to be drawn straight between headlands rather than following every coastal indentation. As a result of such rules, for example, the whole of the Minch between the Outer Hebrides and mainland now forms part of Scotland's internal waters.

International agreement for 12 mile territorial limits was established at the Third United Nations Conference on the Law of the Sea in 1982 as part of the UN Convention on the Law of the Sea (UNCLOS). The distance is similar to Scotland's traditional (and less exact) territorial boundary when Scotland was still an independent country. This was based on rights of exclusive use within the range of vision from sea to land or about 14 miles.[1] Scots lawyers were prominent participants in the European debate during the late 17th century on the limits to be set to territorial seas.

The UN Conventions on the Law of the Sea have also consolidated into customary international law various unilateral claims and other convention agreements over the extent of sovereign rights held by coastal states beyond their 12 mile territorial boundaries. The first main component is an exclusive economic zone extending 200 miles from the 12 mile limit, where it is accepted that coastal states have "sovereign rights for the purposes of exploring and exploiting, conserving and managing the natural resources, whether living or non-living, of the waters superadjacent to the sea-bed, of the sea-bed and its sub-soil".[2]

The second main component is the sovereign rights accepted over the continental shelf for exploring and exploiting its natural resources. These resources are defined as consisting of the mineral and other non-living natural resources of the sea-bed and its subsoil, together with "sedentary species". The nature of sedentary species is not specified but it is taken to include, for example, shellfish and molluscs. The Convention, which provides various formulae for calculating the extent of the continental shelf, can result in sovereign rights extending up to 350 miles beyond the territorial base lines.

Despite these expansions, the international high seas are still much more extensive than the area of seas covered by sovereign rights. The high seas are also still afflicted by over-exploitation despite the attempts of international conventions to regulate their use. This is partially because of the limited powers of enforcement under international law. The expansion of sovereign rights can be claimed to have addressed this to some extent over some of the most heavily used areas of sea, even if the motivation for the expansion was national self-interest. It might be noted in this context that the European Common Fishery Policy establishes common conditions of access to the zones under the marine jurisdiction of member states.

The status of some of the claimed sovereign rights varies with a number of factors, for example, whether they have come fully into force under UN ratification procedures and, in a UK context, whether they have been enacted into domestic law or just accepted as customary international law. Some aspects are a matter of particular detail as, for example, with Rockall, 165 miles west of St Kilda. Britain claimed sovereignty over Rockall in 1955, but does not necessarily enjoy full sovereign rights around it because it is uninhabited territory.

Here, however, there are three main points. Firstly, all these sovereign rights in international seas are of a proprietorial character and based on proximity to sovereign territory. They can thus be viewed as pertinents to that territory and part of that country's system of land tenure. Secondly, within UK legislation, the rights are taken as vested in the Crown and thirdly, the areas (and rights) adjoining Scotland's territorial waters are the subject of Scots law. This latter point had to be specifically clarified for Rockall by the Island of Rockall Act 1972, while it has been done more generally in other provisions (for example, the Continental Shelf Act 1964).

Within Scotland's territorial waters, the sea and sea-bed and associated rights are vested in the Crown in trust for the public. Anciently and traditionally, these were considered to be held inalienably. However, there has been a major shift in judicial opinion (and thus established law) on this over the last 100 years and particularly in recent decades.[3] Some specific rights are still considered held inalienably (for example, navigation and white fishing) and others have been specifically reserved to the Crown (for example, petroleum and gas). However, it is now considered possible for much of the marine environment to be alienated into ownership, even though this appears not to have happened yet beyond the foreshore.[4]

The marine environment therefore involves general public rights, Crown Estate Commission (CEC) administered rights and, potentially, private rights of ownership. Overlying this mix is a very extensive amount of marine legislation involving large numbers of orders and statutory instruments as well as Acts.[5] The modernisation of land tenure provides an opportunity to review and revise this complex and, in terms of sustainable management, unsatisfactory situation. A more straightforward perspective, and one which might provide a more satisfactory basis for a sustainable common property regime, is to separate clearly the roles of the three main parties: Crown, state and private sector. Within this, responsibilities for sovereign marine areas would be the Crown as trustee, the state as manager and the private sector as operator.

One part of establishing such a pattern would be to eliminate the scope for the permanent alienation or long leasing (for example, greater than 20 years) of any part of the sea, sea-bed or its subsoil. Another part would be to remove the CEC from the equation. Their current position as both 'landlord' and 'regulator' might be considered untenable nowadays. The CEC itself aspires to be just a landlord and in the marine environment that role might also be replaced (see below and Chapter 8).[6] Within this proposed arrangement, simply holding the sea in trust for the public would more straightforwardly underpin its management and use through Parliament and its administration either directly by state agencies or more local democratically accountable bodies (see Chapter 8).

The remaining component of the marine environment in this context is the foreshore. Estimates of the overall length of Scotland's foreshore appear to vary because of, for example, the scale at which they were measured. Two contemporary estimates are 10,200 kilometres and 11,770 kilometres.[7] The total for England/Wales is *c.* 7,500 kilometres.

Under the feudal system, the foreshore is treated as an incident of the sea and taken to be held by the Crown, except where evidence can be produced that it has been granted into separate ownership. Under the udal system in much of the Northern Isles, the foreshore is treated as an incident of the land and taken to be held by the occupier of the adjoining land. The extent of udal foreshore is not known, nor is the amount that has been alienated by the Crown over the centuries. The CEC estimates, however, that the Crown still holds approximately 55% of Scotland's foreshore (compared to only 35% in England and Wales despite the absence of any udal tenure there). Special provisions exist in the arrangements for registering titles to land for the CEC to be notified of any claims to foreshore ownership. This enables the CEC to contest any claim it considers unjustified.

Whether someone has a valid grant to the ownership of the foreshore can often depend on attempts to interpret the obscure terms and nuances of ancient titles. Completion of the systematic registration of titles to land should eventually end that. There are also other associated ancient Crown grants in titles which have been or should be replaced by statutory provisions (for example, of port and harbour – see Chapter 10). Also, while modernising land tenure, the capacity of the Crown to alienate the foreshore might be ended. The fact that this has gone on since medieval times is not, of itself, a valid reason for allowing this alienation to continue. There is also the perceived threat of increasing disposal (or long leases) of the foreshore by the CEC, just to increase trading revenues when financial performance has essentially become their measure of success. The likelihood of CEC disposals is reflected in the pattern south of the border and the CEC's progress in operating in the same legal terms in both countries.

In contemporary circumstances, preventing further alienation might be linked to consolidating the Crown's position over the foreshore. This might not amount to re-acquisition except in special public interest instances. However, it might be significant in determining the balance of presumption in the interpretation of uncertain cases that might surface during the final stages of land registration (i.e. when the production of titles is made compulsory).

The case for this consolidation is the dominance of the public interest in the foreshore and associated rights over it. Even under the current legal provisions, the foreshore remains heavily encumbered with public rights when it is in private ownership, including rights of access and recreation, fishing, beaching boats and landing goods.

Indeed, the validity of claiming that what has been alienated actually constitutes 'ownership' might be questioned.

The public rights over the foreshore (and the immediately adjoining strip of land), as with many such aspects of the existing tenure system, require modern expression. This would remove doubts and ambiguities. It would also allow full contemporary recognition of the rights associated with the different aspects of both traditional activities (for example, fishing and beaching boats) and more modern ones (for example, recreational uses, including shooting wildfowl).

These public rights can be seen as linked to the status of the foreshore as an incident of the sea. There is also, at the same time, the opportunity to clarify the pragmatic position where the foreshore can also be seen as an incident of the adjoining land. It might be established more clearly than at present that, subject to public rights, the ownership of that land confers certain *de facto* rights over the foreshore.

In a modernised regime for the foreshore, there might be little pretext for maintaining the direct involvement of the CEC or a successor body. As with other aspects of their current responsibilities, there might be a case for the management of the foreshore becoming a standard local authority responsibility. Local authorities are already empowered to make bye laws over the foreshore and up to 1000 metres out to sea.

Land Surface

The land surface of the mainland and islands of Scotland is bounded by foreshore and the short land frontier with England. The surface area covers 7.88 million hectares, including 0.17 million hectares or 2% defined as open fresh water.[8]

This land surface is the environment of ownership (Chapter 8). The area of this ownership is divided approximately 12%:88% between state and private holdings.[9] The surface area held directly by the Crown hardly features (it is less than 1%), but the key significance of the Crown here is its retained rights and interests in the more than 99% of the surface held from it by others (see Chapter 10). However, there is an opportunity to review and rationalise the areas that are and should be held directly by the Crown, as part of modernising the Crown's place in a reformed system of land tenure in Scotland. At present, there are at least five different situations where the ownership of land is 'attributed' to the Crown.

The first is not directly relevant in this context – the labelling of state-owned land as 'Crown property' because it is held by *HM* government. Neither is the second 'Crown property', because it is the personal estates of the monarch (for example, Balmoral). The question of whether it is appropriate for the monarch (or immediate heirs to the throne) to have personal estates, at least beyond a certain scale, is a separate issue not considered here. A central concern, however, with the personal estates of the monarch is the removal of any prerogative influencing the standards of management on such estates (for example, limiting the application of statutory designation, such as Sites of Special Scientific Interest, on them). The prerogative could be removed straightforwardly by legislation. Another approach would be to require all the monarch's personal lands to be held in trust. Then, by exploiting the separate identities of trusts and beneficiaries under Scots (but not English) law, the trust could be fully liable outwith the beneficary's prerogative.

The third type of 'Crown land' is represented by the Principality of Scotland and held by either the Sovereign or Sovereign's heir by virtue of feudal status. It is presumed this category would disappear with the abolition of feudalism.

The areas which might be considered genuinely appropriate for Crown ownership are included within the final two types of 'Crown land'. These are the parts of the Crown Estate that are managed either by the Crown Estate Commission (CEC) or by some state department or agency. No information seems available on this last category. It includes, for example, Crown commons where Forest Enterprise has taken over the management (for example, The Shooting Greens, Aberdeenshire[10]).

In Scotland, the areas of land managed by the CEC include rural estates, which cover 40,000 hectares (including, for example, Glenlivet), and urban properties in Edinburgh and Glasgow.[11] All these estates and other properties have been purchased this century with the exception of a few *ancient possessions*: five hectares of Princes Street Gardens in Edinburgh and lands at Lythmore (Caithness) and Stirling (which together amount to 600 hectares or 1.5% of the CEC's rural estate in Scotland).

As argued above, there appears little pretext for retaining any of these properties as Crown land except the 'ancient possessions'. The urban properties nearly all date from the last ten years and reflect the ambition of the CEC to be amongst "the UK's leading property investment companies".[12] It is suggested here that the private sector is where that type of ownership and management should be. The CEC could withdraw from the Scottish urban property market easily, as these investments amount to only a small percentage of the value of the urban property held by the CEC in England.

The CEC's rural property in Scotland, while amounting to a third of the CEC's total UK rural acreage, is also of relatively low capital value compared to their holdings in England. At 1.5%, the percentage of ancient possessions and properties acquired before the 20th century is also much lower than in England. The CEC's rural estates in Scotland were not necessarily acquired for just investment reasons (for example, regenerating a rural area was part of the case for purchasing Glenlivet in the 1930s). Again, however, there appears no particular reason why these areas should not be in the private sector – albeit a case might be made that their disposal should involve sub-division into owner occupation or/and a form of community ownership.

The proposition here is that only places of exceptional national significance should be held by the Crown. They are places which, by virtue of their cultural importance, it is considered should be held inalienably in trust for the Scottish nation, represented by the Community of the Realm. Simple examples would be Edinburgh and Stirling Castles and Holyrood Palace.

The identity and ownership of these nationally important sites needs to be clarified. One aspect of this is the position of the National Trust for Scotland (NTS). While the NTS is a voluntary membership association or club, it is the subject of special legislation (1935 and 1947 Acts). This empowers the NTS Council to determine which of the properties acquired by the NTS should be held inalienably for the benefit of the nation. Notwithstanding this, however, the NTS has the power to feu these properties and can, in particular circumstances, dispose of them outright (for example, in the case of a major road realignment).

The NTS's special provisions will need to be revised as part of the abolition of feudal tenure. At that time, it might be questioned whether their special inalienability option is still appropriate. Any properties that are of such national cultural and historical importance to warrant being held inalienably for the benefit of the people of Scotland, might more suitably be vested in the Crown. This would not preclude their continued management by the NTS.

An appropriate portfolio of Crown lands of particular national significance, or 'national shrines', could involve both buildings and landscapes. A case might be made, for example, for a unique mountain area like the Cairngorms Arctic Plateau or particularly significant freshwaters like Loch Ness to be included in such a list.

Currently, the properties that are either already Crown lands or natural choices for that revised status, are managed by a range of bodies (for example, the Crown Estate Commission, Forest Enterprise, Historic Scotland, the National Trust for Scotland, Scottish Natural Heritage). The issue of who should manage them in a reformed situation is not directly a land tenure issue, but a matter of administrative law. The point here is that these 'national shrines' would continue to be held inalienably in trust for the public. The granting of responsibility for their management to a government body or local authority would not amount to alienating them into public/state ownership.

Air Space

Before the 20th century, Scotland and other European countries traditionally claimed that their sovereignty extended to the height of the heavens. The First World War and the use of air power gave a new focus to this and led to the 1919 International Paris Convention for the Regulation of Aerial Navigation. Under this, it was affirmed anew that every sovereign state enjoys complete and exclusive sovereignty over the air space above its territory. This position was reaffirmed at the 1944 Chicago Convention on International Civil Aviation and this remains the basis of international law. However, developments in science and technology continue to make sovereignty over air space an increasingly relative concept, particularly in the upper atmosphere.

The air space above Scotland is part of its territory by virtue of the sovereign rights vested in the Crown as representative of the

Community of the Realm. Over much of the territory's surface, the airspace is above areas retained directly by the Crown (essentially the marine environment). A more important question is the nature of the rights over air space above areas that are in private and state ownership. The current system of land tenure in Scotland still maintains that all owners are granted the ownership of all the air space above their land. One limited exception is situations where ownerships are stacked on top of each other (for example, in tenements or flats).

For centuries, the extent of air space owned above the immediate vicinity of ground level has been irrelevant. In that context, the height of the heavens (or full extent of the air space) was as practical a way as any of defining the area encompassed. Now, however, knowledge and use of, and influence on, that air space is radically different right out to the boundary with outer space. It is hard to see continuing sense in the notion that the pattern of land ownership on the ground should somehow be mirrored in a horizontal cross-cut through the stratosphere miles up. What was essentially irrelevant has become meaningless.

The modernisation of land tenure could reduce the vertical extent of air space conveyed into ownership. There are at least two possible approaches. The first would involve lowering the ceiling to some reasonably definable atmospheric boundary well below the frontier to outer space. The second would involve coming lower still and make air space simply an incident of land ownership.

For the first, the atmosphere has a number of different layers that could provide a somewhat more realistic upper limit to ownership. A principal candidate might be the boundary between the troposphere and stratosphere. This is at about ten kilometres above ground level, compared to the start of outer space at over 600 kilometres. The edge of the troposphere is, of course, a diffuse zone rather than a sharp edge but this is the case for any atmospheric upper limit. Such speculations about heights raise, however, the issue of the significance of ownership at even the more modest level of the troposphere. It might be noted that there are currently only half a dozen man-made structures taller than 500 metres and the tallest (masts) are well below 700 metres.

Over and above any technical constraints in building significantly higher than these masts, the authority to erect any such major structure in Scotland is already subject to overriding public interest controls on development (see Chapter 10). Also, while the right to occupy air space is an important aspect of ownership, that occupation is restricted to being an accessory of buildings. There is no right of ownership to occupy air space without physical attachment. To that extent, air space can be regard as an incident of ownership. Air space should therefore not be listed as part of the territory of ownership.

The position of air space as an incident of surface ownership is reinforced by other aspects, such as the absence of any capacity to dispose of it other than with that surface. As an incident of ownership, there are some parallels with wildlife (see Chapter 10). A fish in a river is an incident of the ownership of that river; air space as an environment is an incident of the ownership of the ground surface. All the rights of ownership related to air space derive from that surface (including, for example, the right to shoot a bird in the sky overhead).

Regarding air space as an incident of ownership relates it more closely in status to air itself. Air is a medium of the environment and, whether above/below ground or inside/outside buildings, has always been held to be *res communis*. It is un-owned except in terms of sovereign rights and, as 'the air we breathe', is a fundamental natural incident of ownership. The interests of ownership in air are related to its quality and consist of rights of self-defence to safeguard the natural quality of air (see Chapter 13). These rights of protection that are conveyed with the ownership of any particular land, are in addition to the more general measures affected in the public interest through Parliament.

As with air, the interests of ownership in air space are primarily rights of protection. These can be against physical encroachment (for example, an overhanging branch) and to secure either the natural or social benefits of ownership (such as light and privacy respectively). These rights, other than those of straightforward physical encroachment from adjoining properties (see Chapter 13), are consistent with the nature of air space as an incident of ownership. They are dependent on a material impact rather than any *de facto* right to object (for example, to a raft of solar panels ten kilometres up).

Thus, rather than the traditional view of air space as a part of ownership, air space in a modernised system of tenure could more realistically remain part of Crown territory. Air space would thus be excluded from ownership as a public interest environment. As with other such areas, while this position derives from the Crown's sovereign rights, the management of air space is a matter for statutory provisions.

Underground

There are similarities between the issues related to ownership above the land surface and below it, including that the concept of ownership is at least as meaningless at the centre of the Earth as it is at the height of the heavens. The centre of the Earth is over ten times further away from the land surface than is outer space. In theory, the size of Scotland's sovereign territory reduces in size as it focuses down towards the centre of the Earth. Even a relatively short distance down in that direction, there is little practical sense in the idea that the land surface pattern of ownership can still be followed.

As with air space, a modernisation of land tenure could consider: firstly, whether to reduce the theoretical extent of ownership from the centre of the Earth back to some closer, more meaningful depth; or secondly, whether to review more fully the whole concept of underground ownership.

An arbitrary depth could be set for the limit of ownership or that limit could be linked to some definable geological boundary, such as the Moho Discontinuity. This is the boundary between the Earth's crust and mantle and is characterised by a distinct change in the character of rocks. The depth of the Moho layer varies, being generally deeper under land than sea, and under Britain is between 27 and 30 kilometres thick. This depth is set in context by the fact that the deepest man-made hole is currently 13 kilometres deep. It is in the USA and is an experimental government geological survey targeted to reach 15 kilometres down. Very few other holes have reached even half this depth. The deepest mine in the world, for example, is less than four kilometres deep.

Limiting the extent of ownership to the depth of the Moho layer (or some such depth) would leave interests deeper than that vested directly in the Crown's sovereign rights. The question then becomes what rights of ownership should be granted out from the Crown between that level and the land surface. In considering this, the situations in the marine and land environments can be distinguished.

The starting position in the marine environment is that the minerals in and under the sea-bed go with the sea-bed itself and are thus retained by the Crown. This should cover without doubt all the territorial sea and associated internal waters and tidal rivers.[13] The main issues are the extent to which these minerals can be granted into ownership by virtue of either the Crown's alienation of areas of sea-bed or of separate mineral rights over parts of it.

It can be argued that the sea-bed should, with the sea itself, remain held inalienably by the Crown in trust for the public (see earlier in this chapter). The case can also be made at the same time that the ownership of minerals in and under the sea-bed should not be considered capable of being owned as a separate tenement from the sea-bed (see Chapter 13). Retrenchment to this regime would mean that only rights of use rather than rights of ownership would be granted out. Thus the exploitation of minerals in and under the sea-bed would all occur under lease or licence. This is the existing situation for a number of specified minerals that are already reserved under any circumstances to the Crown (for example, petroleum and natural gas).

There appears very little case in the public interest for alienating the sea-bed and/or its minerals, other than perhaps the possibility of some larger one-off payment. In comparison to this short-term benefit, however, the proposed regime offers the scope for long-term 'royalties'. These would be likely to be more valuable in the medium to long term. They might also be seen as an appropriate charge on the exploitation of a finite stock of non-renewable resources which make up part of the fabric of Scotland. Such charges could be seen as a way of promoting fuller economic appraisal of actual 'real world' costs (as with, for example, carbon taxes).

The proposed regime also offers a number of other important benefits. These include the capacity to regulate exploration and exploitation in the public interest, as with petroleum and natural gas. It also avoids issues of what actually is conveyed with the ownership of mineral rights (see below) and other potential confusions or conflicts over time between public and ownership interests in the marine environment.

The issue of what is conveyed by a grant of mineral rights has arisen from the historical development of the interpretation that such rights are capable of being owned as a separate tenement (see Chapter 13). This led to debates in the courts on topics such as what are minerals, do they have to be specified and whether only minerals of known commercial significance at the time of the grant were conveyed.[14] Many aspects of these debates are not yet satisfactorily resolved. The Scottish Courts have moved in stages over time to the general conclusion that what is actually conveyed is the ownership of the geological strata or layers and from this, to the view that there is therefore potentially the scope to distinguish and dispose of separately the different geological layers under any piece of land. While this is at odds with the terms of many existing titles to land, it also contrasts with the statutory reservation to the Crown of a number of specified minerals (for example, gold and silver), as well as the vesting of coal in a specific, statutorily constituted body.

The modernisation of land tenure in Scotland provides the opportunity to create a clear and consistent framework for Scotland's underground territory and the exploitation of the minerals (as well as other assets such as thermal heat and subterranean water) contained both under the sea and the land. This could be achieved by a relatively small number of decisions to modify the interpretations that have given rise to unsatisfactory elements in the current arrangements.

Where land is owned, the surface minerals would generally be held by the owner and not be capable of becoming a separate tenement, only the subject of a lease. Then underground, below the surface level, all strata and associated minerals would remain vested in the Crown. This would extinguish minerals as a potential separate tenement.

Underground, the only rights granted out would be rights of use either under lease or licence. This is already the case for the minerals statutorily vested in the Crown. Under ancient Scots legislation, these are gold and silver and could also include copper, lead and tin, although their current status is uncertain.[15] Under modern legislation, they include petroleum, natural gas and uranium. The somewhat anomalous position of the 'ownership' of coal, vested in a state organisation, could be ended by treating it in the same way as the related substances of petroleum and natural gas.

Extending such provisions to cover all underground minerals would recognise the dominant public interest in them as finite non-renewable resources. As it is, the exploitation of any such minerals is already essentially under a licensing system through statutory development controls. In addition, there are also existing statutory provisions empowering, for example, exploration for minerals across any land and requiring the working of any mineral resources, if the government should decide this is required in the national interest.

The granting and operation of rights of use for underground minerals ought not to be administered by the Crown Estate Commissioners, as is the case still with gold and silver. All these matters could be managed, as with petroleum and gas, directly by the state or by some other democratic body acting with its delegated authority. It is also proposed that these rights of use from the Crown should in general only be granted to the owner of the surface. This would not preclude the holder of a Crown mineral lease then making this the subject of a conventional lease to a third party who actually works the minerals. The arrangement would retain a beneficial interest for the owner or owners of surface areas below which minerals are exploited (see Chapter 13).

The retention of all underground minerals as a direct part of Crown territory would make minerals and rights to exploit them an incident of ownership. They would thus (in parallel with wildlife as an incident of ownership) only become owned once they had been mined or in some corresponding way been 'rendered into possession'.

Wildlife and Other Incidents

The territory of Scotland is a natural environment with four main physical dimensions: across the land, out to sea, up in the air and under the ground. Added to all of these is a fifth dimension – wildlife and other natural processes. The components of this fifth dimension are regarded as *incidents* of the territory, in that they do not form part of the physical space itself. Within land tenure they are correspondingly dealt with as incidents of ownership, because they are not by their nature susceptible to ownership as recognised in land tenure.

A simple example is a fish in a river. The river or a length of it may be owned by the Crown, state or someone else, but they do not own the fish. The fish in theory may come and go at will. The fish's presence is incidental to ownership of the river. Of course, as fish also readily illustrate, wild animals can be brought into ownership. However, to achieve that, they will have to be either dead or in captivity – and thus, either way, they are no longer *wild* animals. They will have become wild animals 'rendered into possession'. The position is similar with the other natural incidents that can come with the ownership of land (in its full sense), for example, earthquakes and tides. It may be possible to influence them, even manage or eliminate them, but not own or 'hold' them.

Traditionally, natural process elements such as air and light have been held to be *res communis* as they defy appropriation into ownership. Wild animals, however, have been viewed as *res nullius*, or as having no owner, but with a distinct interpretation of this for a small number of species identified as Royal animals (such as greater whales, see below). Wild plants, on the other hand, are not considered an incident of ownership but a full part of it by virtue of accession (physical attachment) to the land.

This traditional perspective underlies the current place of wildlife and other natural incidents in the present system of land tenure in Scotland. This position dates from before the substantial post-war developments in knowledge and understanding of the natural environment. A central part of this is a more holistic (or ecological) perspective of the environment, with a greater emphasis on natural processes and the ways physical and biological processes interact and merge. During this post-war period, there has also been an increasing build up of legislation relating to wildlife and the natural environment more generally. While this has been seen as very largely administrative law (for example, the Deer (Scotland) Act 1996), it has had many important impacts on rights and responsibilities which spill over into the direct concerns of land tenure (for example, the times of day and seasons of the year when owners need special authorisations to kill deer).

The modernisation of Scotland's system of land tenure would provide an opportunity to ensure the system fully reflects both a contemporary environmental perspective and the implications of related legislation. This is not to suggest that wildlife and other natural processes should now become 'owned'. It would be largely meaningless to propose even that the Crown, as the 'ultimate owner' of the territory, could somehow 'own' them. However, there is a need to clarify the position of wildlife and other natural incidents in relation to the sovereign rights of the Crown and thus the public interest.

The starting point for this is to establish clearly that all rights with respect to wildlife and the other natural incidents of land in Scotland are vested in the first instance in the Crown as Sovereign and so held ultimately in trust for the Community of the Realm. The aim of this perpetual trust can, as with the Crown's wider public responsibilities for the territory as a whole, be construed as the sustainable management or stewardship of the natural wealth and assets involved for the social, economic and environmental benefit of the people of Scotland.

The Crown's position as the source of all rights of management and use over Scotland's wildlife and other natural incidents is entrenched in both the external and internal aspects of sovereignty (see Chapter 5). Internationally, sovereignty is the basis of control over territory and with it, the natural incidents of that territory. It is the recognised authority or right to defend the territory and its incidents against external influences arising from within other jurisdictions, whether by design or default. Correspondingly, sovereignty carries the rights of use and enjoyment and, domestically, there is no authority over the territory except through the Crown. Thus, all owners and occupiers, whether state or private, only derive rights of management and use from that authority. In the Scottish constitution, with the sovereignty of the people and not of parliament, it is these sovereign rights of the Crown that empowers parliament to legislate over relevant topics in the public interest.

It might also be noted that it is a matter of responsibilities as well as rights. Wildlife and other natural incidents are not all beneficial (for example, 'pest' and 'disease' species, floods or earthquakes). The Crown's position can also be seen as the basis of a public responsibility to help those unduly disadvantaged through no actions of their own by wildlife and natural incidents. However, the key point is that for wildlife and other natural incidents, as for other elements of territory, there are core principles to which Parliament is giving expression at any point in time.

This parliamentary framework of who can do what, where, when and how straddles the area from the ground rules of land tenure to the practicalities of administrative law. These latter considerations are the day-to-day arena of concern, but clarifying the Crown's position establishes that the starting point in this ongoing debate is the public interest. The ambiguity that has become associated with *res nullius* (for example, that the first claim or right to take wildlife 'belongs' to the owners of land) is replaced by full recognition that the management of wildlife is a common property regime (*res communis*).

This position is most obvious in the marine environment, notably through the public right of fishing as regulated by statute. Modernisation of land tenure provides the opportunity to develop this to encompass all wildlife on a consistent basis. This should include removal of the last vestiges of the notion of Royal animals. *Greater whales*, for example, are considered to have this status but there is no legal clarity about which species might be involved or about what the implications might be. Whales, as with all other species, should be straightforwardly covered by statutory provisions.

Extinction altogether of the category of Royal animals should be linked to the removal of rights to any particular animals from the regalia minora, for example, the capacity of the Crown to make separate grants over the ownership of salmon fishings and of rights to oyster and mussel beds. At the same time, automatic public rights to particular species should also be curtailed (for example, freshwater mussels). Open access to resources can lead to their over-exploitation ('the tragedy of the commons'), and does not provide the basis of sustainable common property regimes.

With freshwater mussels, the question is not necessarily about who has the right of 'use'. The issue is how such a public right is regulated and this has recently been reformed by statute. However, the freshwater mussel is an exception as a species subject to a public right even over land that is in private ownership. It appears to be the only species in this position in the land/freshwater environment. Public rights to take wild animals are essentially confined to the marine environment, including the foreshore and tidal waters. There they coincide with Crown land. Similar general rights over wild animals might exist in the land/freshwater environment over Crown Commons, but the existence and operation of these is not clear at present.[16]

Other public rights are traditionally claimed. There is a widespread belief in Scotland, for example, that there is a public right to fish for brown trout in all freshwater rivers and streams.[17] While this was historically the case, by the 19th century the law had overtaken it and granted an exclusive right of trout fishing to the proprietors of the water. The rights of owners in wild brown trout and other wild fresh water fishes have also been significantly increased relatively recently (by the Freshwater & Salmon Fisheries (Scotland) Act 1976). However, there would be no particular practical difficulty in implementing an effectively managed and sustainable public right to take wild brown trout in freshwaters.[18] Also, it would arise in part if the public rights in tidal rivers were reinstated over the full navigable lengths of any such rivers (see Chapter 10). The issues are about the distribution of rights, rather than technical difficulties necessitating a particular choice.

More generally, the right to take wild animals was not associated historically with the ownership of the land where they are taken. However, with the exceptions of the public right to freshwater oysters and the status of salmon fishings as a separate tenement, rights over wild animals are now conveyed with titles to land as incidents of ownership. The core issue is therefore the terms and conditions of such a grant. This includes both the general principles deriving from Crown rights over wild animals and the specific framework applied by Parliament at any time.

The position of wild plants is different. For much longer historically, rights over these have been taken as an integral part of the ownership of land. The distinction has been based essentially on the mobility of wild animals compared to the physical attachment of wild plants to the land. Biologically, this distinction is not very accurate. The mobility of some plants is particularly obvious in the marine environment. However, most attention has focused on 'sedentary animals' (for example, shellfish such as oysters and clams) and using their sedentary nature to claim greater rights over them than can be held for other wild animals. This has been at the national level with, for example, claims through international law of the sea conventions to sedentary animals (unspecified) outwith territorial waters (see earlier this chapter) and at the ownership level, claims in court over species that exhibit significant attachment for at least part of their life (for example, whelks).

The acceptance of rights over wild plants as part of ownership is, at a general level, a common sense position. However, it is not a rule that need necessarily apply to all species. In many European countries, for example, there are public rights to certain species of wild plants, notably for berries and fungi. In addition, the conveyancing of rights of wild plants with ownership should not be taken to imply that wild plants are any different in their actual legal status from wild animals. At a simple level, there is a contradiction between calling them wild plants whilst saying they are the property of the owner of the land. What is conveyed is rights over them, not the plants themselves.

For wild plants as for wild animals, there is a fuller sense to being 'rendered into possession' than just the fact that they occur within an owner's property. Similarly, just as the law is capable of recognising differences in rights and responsibilities between wild and domestic animals, so the law can recognise distinctions between wild and cultivated plants.

In this sense, wild plants and wild animals ought both to be held to be *res communis*. This is a conclusion that might also be reached by a different route. It could be held that the culminative affect of legislation dealing with wildlife over recent decades has been effectively to *nationalise* wild plants (see Chapter 10). The restrictions imposed by statute on the rights over plants of land owners can be seen to amount to something equivalent to the way planning laws nationalised the right of development. In the modernisation of land tenure in Scotland, fuller recognition of the wildness of wild plants would not necessarily imply any conversion or transfer of owners' rights to public rights. However, it would clarify the balance of presumption between public and private interests in defining the terms and conditions attached to ownership.

CHAPTER TEN

Rights Retained in the Public Interest

Rights of Recovery

Much of Scotland is granted out from the Crown into ownership. Grants are conveyed by titles to land and confer on the owner (title holder) all the basic rights of ownership (for example, security and peaceful enjoyment, succession and disposal, use and lease – see Section 4). The Crown has always, however, retained certain rights in the public interest over the properties granted out. The ownership conferred is not absolute and the rights retained and granted can be seen as the terms and conditions of ownership.

At present, after centuries of the present system, there are many aspects of the rights that the Crown retains that are either archaic or unclear. The modernisation of land tenure would provide an opportunity to rationalise and consolidate these Crown rights. One approach is to view these Crown rights as grouped into a number of broad categories that represent the key principles determining the basic scope of ownership. Each of these could then be given practical expression through Parliament and revised as necessary by Parliament from time to time.

Some of the main categories of retained rights are illustrated in this chapter. Amongst them, the natural starting point might be labelled 'rights of recovery'. These involve the capacity of the Crown in the public interest to recover land (and associated incidents of land) that has been granted out.

The most basic amongst these rights of recovery is that any land that is clearly established to have no owner automatically reverts to the Crown. This situation arises most commonly where no heir can be traced but, in future, with comprehensive digitised mapping of ownership, may arise where areas that were presumed granted out are found to have no owner. While, in practice, there are statutory arrangements to settle the fate of any such areas, their initial reversion to the Crown follows from the Crown's fundamental position as the ultimate source of ownership (see Chapter 5).

This principle of reversion to the Crown when there is no owner extends to such ownerless incidents of land as treasure trove, lost property and wrecks. 'Treasure' has come to be defined broadly and dovetails with definitions of lost property. Similarly, 'wrecks' is now a general term including aircraft and the like. These broad definitions provide for a comprehensive framework for dealing with these 'incidents'. While this framework should again be covered by statutory arrangements, the Crown's basic right allows, for example, treasure or other incidents of national significance to be retained in public ownership. Similarly, this 'national interest' underpins, for example, dealing pre-emptively with wrecks (salvage operations to prevent wrecks). Importantly, it also provides the basic parameters for interpreting and responding to any incidents that may arise beyond the scope of the current statutory provisions.

The Crown's rights of recovery extend from the passive rights identified above, to rights involving direct intervention to resume land. These rights of recovery are, for example, the foundation of compulsory purchase in the public interest. The rights might also be taken to include a Crown right of pre-emption to acquire land in the national interest when the land is being sold (see page 137).

The Crown's powers of resumption are reflected in the dictum that ownership gives way to the public interest (as explained in Chapter 6). While the exercise of these rights may most commonly be to achieve some constructive public purpose, they also include the resumption of land as a punitive measure. Traditionally, this has been seen principally as a response to treason, which is in the final analysis against the Crown. In a modernised system of land tenure, this Crown right of resumption or confiscation could also provide a measure of last resort against the management of land that is viewed, in a wider sense, as betraying the public interest (see page 132).

Rights of Passage

The current system of land tenure in Scotland has always recognised the public right of navigation in Scotland's territorial waters, associated internal waters and tidal rivers. This legally entrenched 'freedom to roam' also covers the foreshore and extends up freshwater rivers that are legally established as 'navigable'. A reform of land tenure provides the opportunity to clarify and modernise aspects of this public right. This includes, for example, the range and nature of the activities associated with such rights of public access. With navigable rivers, it could include a modern definition determining which rivers and other water bodies are considered navigable.

The public right of navigation over the marine waters is held over territory that is all retained by the Crown. The same public rights of passage up navigable rivers and on the foreshore are, or can be, over land granted out into ownership. However, the main issue with public rights of passage is their extent more generally over land granted into ownership.

Public rights of passage over such land must inevitably be more conditional, by virtue of the fact that they are over land 'owned' by some particular party other than the Crown. However, it might still be reasonable to conclude that the general right of passage over Scotland's marine territory is also held over the rest of Scotland's territory or land. The retention of this general right can be seen in terms of both the specific rights in law of public access over parts of the land and the interpretation that can be put on existing access provisions in law over land generally.

The specific rights of public access include, in addition to those associated with the foreshore and navigable rivers, those governing public highways ('the Queen's highway') and public rights of way. These provide for a comprehensive and secure, but flexible, network of public routes over Scotland's land between public places. A modernisation of land tenure offers the opportunity both to recognise more clearly and to rationalise this fundamental framework of main public routes. This could be linked to removing a number of ancient Crown rights that are related to public access, such as grants to operate ferries, establish ports and harbours, and to hold fairs and markets. These rights have already been largely replaced by statutory provisions, and the remaining elements should be brought fully under statutory provisions and regulated through either central or local government.

The overall objective should be that there is a dominant principle of a right of passage over land held in trust for the people of Scotland and to which Parliament gives practical expression. Extensive legislation already deals with public highways. The Crown right of passage can be seen as empowering the compulsory provisions associated with establishing (or extinguishing) public roads and other public routes such as bridges, railways and canals. Some legacies still remain that might be removed as unnecessary complications, such as the continued private ownership of the solum under some public roads.

There is a greater need to modernise the law with respect to public rights of way, including aspects where judicial presumption should be replaced with statutory provision. The continuing legal assumption that public rights of way can be established by Crown grants,[1] should become integrated into the wider statutory framework for the creation of public paths and long distance routes. The position of rights of ways, including the different forms of travel that can be used on them, should also dovetail with the public highways provisions.

Overall, existing rights held by the Crown and implemented through Parliament can be relatively easily developed as an integrated, comprehensive and flexible framework for public routes. However, its counterpart, an unambiguous general right held in trust by the Crown of public access over land, has yet to be fully recognised in either statutory or judicial law.

This 'freedom to roam' needs to be conditional over owned land. It should be seen as a balance between, on the one hand, public rights of passage and peaceful enjoyment and, on the other, private rights of privacy and protection from material damage to property or livelihood. The practicality of such a balance is demonstrated by the legal codes governing such arrangements in Scandinavian and other European countries. An initial basis for an equivalent statutory code in Scotland could be the Access Concordat that has been agreed between the main groups representing hill-walking and landowning interests in Scotland.

This general right involves passive access (i.e. following one's route without engaging in other potentially disruptive activities, which is equivalent to the passive right of passage of foreign vessels through Scottish territorial waters). Trespass, to the limited extent that it has legal meaning in Scotland and is relevent in this context, is defined by activities rather than simply presence. Thus, while legislation such as the Trespass (Scotland) Act 1865 needs modernised and liberalised in certain specific circumstances, activities such as camping and lighting a fire do not form part of the basic public right of access.

A *de facto* freedom to roam existed in Scotland historically and the continued existence of such a public right of passage is not precluded by existing laws. However, over the last 150 to 200 years and notably during the last 30 years, the interpretation and representation of the law has been unsympathetic to such a right and created the current ambiguity.[2] Within this, in general terms, anyone is still allowed anywhere under the law without offence, but owners have become empowered to ask them to leave their property without the requirement of any legitimate reason or cause.

The shift away from the historical position could reflect in part the balance of sympathy amongst those responsible for establishing and representing legal opinion. While the shift has been significant, it has been modest compared to many similar shifts within land tenure over the same general period (for example, the slide of hunting rights from being a universal right to a privilege or incident of ownership to a leaseable commodity towards becoming a separate tenement – see Chapter 14). Another factor has been the influence of English law, with its particular 'hostility' toward public access and under which mere presence counts as trespass and is an offence.

With the current position in Scotland more ambiguous in its legal representation and interpretation than its day-to-day practice, the traditional freedom to roam can be still construed as a public right of passage. Modern circumstances require, however, that this right is clearly defined in legislation and potentially supported by a civil code. Within this, an owner would need a justifiable reason to require someone to leave their land.

Thus, in a modernised system of land tenure in Scotland, it might be anticipated that the ownership of land would be subject to rights held in trust by the Crown that provided for, firstly, a universal but conditional right of public access over all owned land and, secondly, a comprehensive framework of specific measures for secure public routes.

Rights of Stewardship

The Crown, by virtue of the sovereign rights it holds in trust for the public, has a responsibility for the management of Scotland's territory and its natural wealth and resources. This responsibility can be equated with stewardship (as explained in Chapter 4). To meet this responsibility, it is necessary for the Crown to retain appropriate rights of the stewardship over land granted out into ownership. This involves the capacity to determine the overall scope of the rights of use and management held by owners – in other words, the basic nature of what owners can or can not do with their land.

The main rights involved in stewardship can be related to *conservation and development*. There is still some perceptual legacy from narrow and sectoral conflicts over land use, that conservation and development may be inherently opposed terms. However, they are used here as two sides of the same coin, in the broader sense of conserving (or maintaining) what is sufficiently valued and developing (or changing) the rest appropriately.

The modernisation of land tenure in Scotland provides the opportunity to establish clearly that all land granted out from the Crown is held conditionally under the overall requirements of the conservation and development of land and other natural resources in the public interest, where that public interest is represented by the Crown and determined by Parliament from time to time.

This conditional position is in line with the traditional dictum that owners can do what they like with their land, subject to their title and the general laws of the land. However, the modernisation of land tenure is likely to result in a more balanced perspective on this. Since the heyday of Victorian landownership, by when title conditions had been weakened and statutory controls were still limited, the qualifying statements in the dictum have often been under-represented by landowning interests – as illustrated in recent years by statements from Conservative government ministers, such as Lord Lindsay, asserting without qualification that it is up to land owners what they do with their land.[3]

The modernisation should also seek to reconcile the disparate ways title and statutory conditions have evolved over the last hundred years or more. The removal of feudal titles and their replacement by modern, standard titles should result in land being held subject to a relatively small number of basic principles, which are then interpreted and implemented by Parliament. The conservation and development principles which underpin the rights of stewardship retained by the Crown should also set a new or clearer benchmark for what might be considered to constitute a 'taking' (a regulation that takes away a right of ownership and so gives rise to a claim for compensation – as explained in Chapter 6).

The principles of conservation and development are based on and derived from the mixture of the controls inherent in Scotland's feudal tenure (rights in exchange for responsibilities) and more recent related legislation (in particular starting with the planning and countryside acts passed immediately post World War II). Controls and responsibilities for the buildings and similar developments preceded those related to the natural environment, but these two aspects might be considered ripe for a new synthesis (as explained below).

The 19th century use of feudal superiorities to control patterns of urban development was followed by the emergence of the statutory planning system, as first consolidated in the Town and Country Planning (Scotland) Act 1947. The system was created as a democratically accountable instrument of government to be "a means of restricting private land use rights in the interests of the community as a whole".[4] The aim of the system is to bring all "development" of land within its scope, where development results in either some material physical change or a material change in use. Development is thus defined very widely (for example, "the carrying out of building, engineering, mining or other operations in, on, over or under land, or the making of a material change in the use of any buildings or other land" (1947 Act)). Exemptions can exist at any time (for example, forestry operations), but they are simply exemptions and not outwith the principle and scope of planning as a statutory system of control. The system is "neither a static nor a neutral system of rules, and the balance which it sets between private and public interest, and between the different institutions representing the public interest, is constantly changing".[5] However, control in the public interest over the development of land remains the enduring principle.

It is generally held that the introduction of the statutory planning system "nationalised the right of development".[6] This is the consequence of the legislation rather than its stated wording. The consequence could be seen not so much as 'nationalisation', but as Parliament interpreting and implementing one of the basic retained Crown rights of stewardship – the principle of control over development in the public interest.

The modernisation of land tenure in Scotland provides the opportunity to consolidate this public interest control over development. There are elements that could be clarified. In particular, it could be established more clearly that the system is not simply a qualification to the private property right of development, but that the right of development is a privilege of ownership that can only be exercised with the sanction of the state.[7] A number of public interest benefits would flow from this clarification. It would, for example, make it clear that the onus in the development process is on the developers to establish the acceptability of their proposals, rather than for planning authorities to demonstrate why any particular development should be refused permission. This in turn would enable the precautionary principle to be fully integrated into the statutory planning system, in line with the government's international commitments, for example, from the Earth Summit in Rio in 1992.[8]

The planning system's involvement with the concerns of environmental conservation has already expanded rapidly over recent decades. The public interest in such matters has made them a central strand of this statutory system, despite many shortcomings that could be listed (for example, the extent to which the expansion of forestry and erection of agricultural buildings are exempt from planning controls). Public interest has also led to major developments in both statutory measures relating to the natural environment and other planning laws. The National Parks and Access to the Countryside Act 1949 can be viewed as a consolidating precursor to many aspects of this legislative strand, in much the same way as the 1947 Planning Act was for development control.

Elements of this development in environmental legislation can be traced back to ancient origins (for example, medieval acts protecting species for hunting) or key legislation in the 19th century (for example, acts promoting bird conservation and pollution control). However, the whole sector has gone through a radical change of gear over the last 50 years in both the amount of legislation and range of topics covered. In this process, legislation has long since moved from dealing with specific species and selected activities, to extensive provisions for all species and types of natural resource management and environmental regulation. The scope of this legislation, and the standards it requires, is also likely to continue to develop (for example, legislation setting essentially the same 'humanitarian' standards for the treatment of wild animals as for domestic animals, as has been proposed in private members' bills in the House of Commons).

Given the extent and nature of the existing laws, the point may have been reached where, if the planning system is seen as having nationalised the right of development, the cumulative impact of wildlife and environmental legislation might be considered to have nationalised the responsibilities of conservation. This conclusion recognises that the control of developments and the requirements of conservation are both encompassed within statutory frameworks that restrict the land use rights of ownership in the interests of the community as a whole.

That this view is not widely recognised does not of itself reduce the importance of suggesting the conclusion. Much of the key legislation involved is still very recent and there is no clear perspective yet on this related legislation as a coherent and integrated framework (as is the case with the planning system with all its different dimensions and ramifications). There is considerable scope for developing such a consolidating framework as part of modernising land tenure in Scotland. A simple example can be seen in the statutory provisions for killing or capturing wild animals – under these, all owners are obliged to take some species, are allowed to choose to take some other species, require a state licence to take others and are prohibited from taking all the rest. This illustrates not only a controlling statutory framework, but also an element of statutory responsibility – a requirement to act or acquiesce to action by others in certain circumstances.

There is a need to establish more clearly in modernising land tenure that this statutory responsibility extends to the management of all wild animals, associated habitats and natural processes. Their management is not simply a matter of some moral responsibility (for example, as was argued in recent debates on new deer legislation for Scotland by those seeking to resist a statutory responsibility to control deer numbers). A clear recognition has also developed over recent years that neglect is still an act of management and that simply refraining from carrying out damaging operations may not adequately meet the responsibilities that go with the ownership of land.

A requirement to take positive action to protect defined environmental assets in the public interest is, however, one aimed at maintaining the status quo rather than producing enhancement. There is essentially no distinction between the requirement to protect a unique habitat or a historic building, although at present there is some unevenness in the greater statutory powers available to protect the built environment in comparison to the natural environment.

It should be recognised that, overall, the rights of stewardship are the dominant interest in the management and use of both the natural and man-made environment. These rights are not merely a qualification of the rights of ownership, but should set the terms and conditions of the privileges of management and use that are conveyed with ownership.

The stewardship of land has social as well as environmental dimensions. However, good stewardship can be viewed in a broader context as the environmental equivalent to good citizenship. They are both goals to aspire to, not constraints to be resented.

Rights of Charges

The final category of rights illustrated here as retained over all land by the Crown in trust for the people of Scotland, is the right to raise charges on land. The ownership of land in Scotland has always been subject to charges and duties in one form or other under the current long-standing system of land tenure. The provision of goods and services in exchange for ownership was inherent in the reciprocal nature of feudalism from the start. The survival of the last vestiges of feu duties is a continuing reminder of this. Feu duties also reflect

the way charges or duties on the ownership of land have all essentially become a matter of monetary payments.

The abolition of feudal tenure would do away with feu duties and
any other charges and duties by one owner over another that can
still be associated with superiorities (see Chapter 13). The scope for
any forms of private charges by owners on other owners might then
also be precluded from a reformed system. In contrast to this, the
possession of a title to land or heritable property might continue to
carry a liability to public charges (as with, for example, the current
Council Tax). The right to make charges on the ownership of land
would be retained by the Crown as a matter of principle and be
inherent in the granting of a title. The issue of whether any charges
are raised or what their nature and rates might be, would then be a
matter determined at any point in time by the democratic processes
of government.

The retention of this right to make public charges would legit-
imise them as a part of land tenure. However, the incorporation of
this principle into a reformed system should define its key parameters. This would distinguish between the general power of government to raise taxes and the aspects of that which are considered a
legitimate component of the land tenure system, as discussed below.

Historically, charges on land were central to national revenues.
This was based on the close relationship between land and wealth.
Over the centuries broader aspects of wealth became the focus of
taxation (for example, the start of income tax in 1799). During the
same period, two characteristic features of public charges on land
became more explicitly established. These features still survive and
might form the main parameters of public charges in a reformed
system of land tenure.

The first of these features is that charges on land are payments in
exchange for something – for services (for example, police and fire
services) or other benefits incidental to the ownership of land (for
example, the right to hunt certain species of wildlife). This principle
defines clearly that the scope of charges *within* the land tenure
system *per se* does not include taxes to promote the redistribution of
wealth or land. Clearly, redistributional taxation will remain within
the power of government, but it would not be as a component of the
land tenure system.

The second feature is that charges on land are raised for *local* rather than central government. At present, while the proportion of local authority revenue raised locally has been reduced markedly, that proportion is still raised by charges on land through the Council Tax and related rates. The Council Tax is paid in exchange for services. The fact that it is currently based on buildings does not preclude an expansion to levy rates on land as such. It is notable, for example, that the owners of more extensive areas of land benefit from local services in ways that are not reflected in the current basis of the Council Tax. These include, for example, support from fire services to control muirburn or moorland fires started by owners which get out of control.

The charges that might be raised in exchange for the other incidental benefits of ownership are broader and less clear cut in their scope. Examples might span from annual charges on sporting rights to levying a charge at the point of sale on enhanced capital values of properties as a result of public investment (for example, the development value of land going up due to the local authority providing local water and sewerage services nearby). This latter approach was attempted by the former Community Land Tax and the legitimate public interest in these enhanced values is still an important issue to be addressed.[9]

Sporting rates can be seen as a charge for the privilege of taking various species of wildlife, where that privilege is an incident of ownership and the wildlife is a public resource. This charge could thus be viewed as a 'royalty' on a renewable rather than non-renewable natural resource. Historically, sporting rates were very important to local revenues in many areas.[10] They have not been charged since the early 1990s, but they were charged whether the resources are exploited or not. This can be related to wider ideas, such as those of the 19th century reformer Henry George and his proposals for taxing land values as an incentive to appropriate land use.

Sporting rates also illustrate the proposition that charges for incident benefits should, like any charges for services, be fair and not punitive. Charges should also be seen to encourage good management. This was often a matter of debate with sporting rates when they were still charged. However, there is no reason why such local charges should not be a useful tool in encouraging good management. They could be complementary to other existing public payments (for example, land management grants) and national tax concessions (for example, exemption from Inheritance Tax in exchange for public access) that are intended to achieve the same overall objective.

Conclusions from Section 3

Chapter 7 Scotland's Sovereign Lands

• Scotland's land tenure system encompasses the whole territory of Scotland – all its land and surrounding territorial seas, together with all the ground below and airspace above these areas.

• The sovereign rights from which Scotland's system of land tenure derives also confer various rights and responsibilities under international law that extend beyond Scotland's territorial boundaries.

Chapter 8 The Crown Estate

• Clearer recognition could be given to the public interest in those parts of Scotland's territory held directly in trust for the people of Scotland in the Crown's name and under the authority of Parliament.

• The responsibilities of the Crown Estate Commission in Scotland could be constituted in Scots law and transferred to democratically accountable bodies.

Chapter 9 Natural Assets Held by the Public

• The whole of the marine environment could continue to be held directly in trust for the people of Scotland while, on land, this status could be limited to a few nationally important sites.

• Realistic limits could be set to the extent of rights that go with land ownership above and below ground, and the rights of the public interest over wildlife could be formally recognised in Scots law.

Chapter 10 Rights Retained in the Public Interest

• The rights retained in the Crown's name over all the land owned, whether by public bodies or private persons, establish the conditional nature of land ownership in Scotland.

• These public rights can be grouped into several broad categories and within each, there is scope to both rationalise and consolidate the extent and nature of the rights involved.

SECTION FOUR
The Ownership of Land

CHAPTER ELEVEN

Rights to Own and Dispose of Land

This chapter considers the issue of who can own land in Scotland by examining the types of natural and legal persons entitled to hold a title to land. It also considers the degree of freedom owners have to hand on, sell or in other ways dispose of their land to others.

Entitlement

Scotland's system of land tenure can be considered to have, in the final analysis, three core ingredients: sovereignty, democracy and ownership. The system is founded upon the sovereign rights associated with the Crown in Scotland. These rights are interpreted and implemented through the democratic process of Parliament – and the ownership of property, including land, is one of the cornerstones of that democracy (see Chapter 3).

A basic divide in Scotland's land tenure system is between the rights and interests of the Crown and those of ownership. The areas held directly by the Crown set the land in ownership within an overall physical context. The rights and interests retained by the Crown in all the land held by owners then set the basic terms and conditions governing the rights and interests that go with ownership. Within that framework, ownership can be defined as conveying certain basic rights and interests to the owners of land.

Land is owned by virtue of possessing a valid title to it and, at one level, ownership can be equated simply with titleholding (see Chapter 7). The abolition of feudal tenure offers the opportunity, in the first instance, to rationalise this foundation to ownership. All titles to land would be held direct under the Crown through a single method of holding or owning land and all titles would be recorded in a comprehensive and state guaranteed register of titles to land (see Chapter 7).

These reforms could also encompass refinements to the definitions of the natural and legal persons who can hold titles to land in
Scotland (see below). Beyond that, there is the opportunity to review
and modernise the basic rights and interests that all owners are
entitled to enjoy by virtue of their title to land. Crucial components
of this entitlement are the legal rights and interests represented by
concepts such as 'peaceful enjoyment' and 'freedom and quietness'
(as explained in Chapter 6). These provide owners with what is
deemed a legitimate counter-balance to the rights and interests of the
Crown and the state over land.

Ownership is also defined by a range of other 'real rights', such
as the authority to lease land or alienate it to others. These rights
and interests, which involve the relationships both between owners
and between them and others, should all come within the scope of
modernising Scotland's system of land tenure. At present, like other
components of Scotland's existing system of land tenure, these rights
and interests of ownership contain archaic elements, areas of uncertainty and aspects that could be modernised to improve both the
overall position of owners and the balance between public and
private interests.

Entitled Persons

In Scotland, as in all other countries, there are legal limits as to who
is entitled to own land. Reform of the system of land tenure in
Scotland provides the opportunity to review these limitations. The
starting point for this might be the general democratic principle that
no particular persons or types of persons should be precluded from
holding a title to land in Scotland, except where there is an adequate
case in the public interest.

'Persons' in this context can be divided into natural persons
(human beings) and legal persons (entities such as limited companies
and other corporate bodies granted personality in Scots law). A
distinction can also be made between those categories of persons of
either type who are debarred from acquiring a title at all and those
who, due to some change in circumstances, become disqualified
from continuing to hold a title.

The first requirement for entitlement is general contractual
capacity. Thus, a natural person can be precluded from acquiring a

title by insanity (being of unsound mind) as that is defined under Scots law. Partial preclusion also results from 'nonage', with restrictions on the capacity of children to acquire and dispose of land. With legal persons, associations and partnerships do not have sufficient legal identity in Scots law to hold titles in their own right (titles are held in the names of the office-bearers and partners respectively). Companies and trusts do have a legal identity that enables them to hold titles, subject in each case to the provisions of their own constitutions. Trusts in particular have been important as owners of land in Scotland since the 17th century and continue to be widely used as a way of holding land.[1]

In each of the cases above (insanity, nonage, legal personality), it needs to be clearly established that these are as defined in Scots law. At present, there can be doubt in some instances whether the laws of another country apply, where a natural person may be a national or where a legal person may have the capacity to own land.

This should also be linked to requirements of traceability and accountability in Scots law, based on a legally responsible person within Scotland. There is an important public interest in both being able to identify and contact title holders and readily obtain their authority (for example, for public and private utilities dealing with services such as electricity, water and gas), and also in being able to take action against them if necessary within Scotland's jurisdiction. Requirements of registration and disclosure would have parallels with the current provisions of the Companies Act for companies operating in the UK. The extra need for this traceability and accountability has grown with increasing mobility in the modern world and the complexity of arrangements that can be involved in the identity of a legal person. Trusts are a particular case, where issues can arise over the identities of the trustees and beneficiaries (for the relationship between trustees and beneficiaries see page 141).

The disqualification of appropriately entitled persons from entitlement to hold a title to land in Scotland needs to be distinguished from the general ways titles can be lost involuntarily. These latter include, firstly, circumstances where a title was acquired improperly, for example, from someone who was not fully responsible for their actions (for example, a nonage or temporarily drunk person) or by fraud or undue coercion. They also include, secondly, compulsory purchase in the public interest, common property where the division of this can be initiated by another, bankruptcy where this leads to action by debtors or debts more generally where land has been used as a security.

More directly, disqualification can result from loss of contractual capacity (for example, being declared insane or becoming 'presumed dead' in law). This type of disqualification can also be temporary (for example, taking into custody the property of 'alien enemies' at times of war). The confiscation of estates by the State after the 1745–6 Jacobite Rebellion was the last episode to date in a long history of forfeiture of titles for treason. However, being convicted of treason might still be defined as grounds for disqualification.[2]

Thus, at present, while a particular title can be lost for a variety of reasons (because it was obtained by fraud, compulsory purchase, etc), the only grounds for an overall disqualification on holding a title to land are madness, treason or 'presumed death'. However, it might be argued that there should be a last-resort power for government to disqualify a particular person (natural or legal) on the basis that they are not *competent* to own land. For this, competence would need to be defined in the laws of land tenure, rather than simply the laws of contract. It would, however, be parallel to the way individuals can be, for example, barred at law from being company directors. There is no direct precedent for standards of ownership as a basis for disqualification. However, the 1948 Agriculture (Scotland) Act provided, for example, important powers for land to be removed from owners where it was not being used appropriately. Most of these powers in the 1948 Act have been repealed, but standards of resource use can still, for example, allow a landlord to remove a tenant for a breach of 'good husbandry'. This is seen as a legitimate concern of the lease granter (landlord) over the leaseholder (tenant). There might be considered, similarly, a legitimate concern of the title granter (Crown) over the title holder (owner).

There are many issues to be explored in considering the idea of the ultimate sanction of disqualification. However, it would clearly only be warranted where there was a definite and substantial public interest and might be related to the idea of an overall statutory responsibility for sound (sustainable) resource use as a condition of title holding. It would act as a long-stop after the regulation of the individual sectors of resource use by Parliament and associated public bodies.

Succession

An authority to pass on, bequeath, sell or otherwise dispose of land to a particular person or persons (natural or legal), has long been one of the most basic rights of land ownership in Scotland. In particular, the arrangements governing the succession to land in Scotland, have been one of the defining characteristics of Scotland's system of feudal tenure.

The intimacy of this link is illustrated by the long-standing legal use of 'heritable property' to describe land as a distinct form of property and the fact that the laws of succession are central to defining the difference between land and other, moveable property. Any land owner (title holder) is still technically known as a Heritor, while Heritage is another term that continues to be used for property in the form of lands and buildings (as in 'lands and heritages'). This use of heritage, however, is being overtaken by contemporary terms such as natural heritage and cultural heritage, which refer to a public inheritance rather than the private property of heritors. These labels (heritable, heritage, heritor) might all now be considered redundant, particularly since the reforms to the laws of succession in 1964 (see below) and given the availability, when they are required, of modern technical equivalents (for example, immoveable property and title holder).

However, the reform of Scotland's system of land tenure provides a wider opportunity than just replacing terminology, to ensure that the arrangements governing succession in land tenure are suitably equitable and expedient to match society's contemporary values and expectations. The scope for modernisation is perhaps readily illustrated by the survival of entails – a legal arrangement that safeguards the succession of land to a prescribed line of heirs. This meant, for example, that if a land owner became bankrupt their estate would pass to their successor and escape being sold to meet the demands of creditors.

The laws of entail were crucially important in the build up and subsequent maintenance of large estates in Scotland from the 17th to 19th centuries.[3] The significance of entails has declined markedly this century. The right to create new entails was abolished in 1914 and, while there has always been some scope to 'break' entails, there have been a number of statutory provisions this century to make this easier. It was estimated in the 1960s that there were still around 2000 entailed estates, while now it may be down to a few hundred.[4]

The final abolition of the laws of entail would be relatively straightforward to legislate for. It is not just a matter of removing an anachronistic remnant of feudalism, but warranted by social justice. Entails, for example, work against the natural line of succession and are also at odds with the normal provisions in respect of other property for an entitlement to legal shares for spouses and issue (children).

'Spouses and issue' are also involved in the other main issue involving the succession to land. Succession within Scotland's feudal tenure has been based in law on primogeniture (inheritance by the eldest male descendant). This principle derives from the start of feudalism in Scotland and can be related to the monarchs at that time establishing their line of succession to the Crown.[5] The influence of primogeniture since then has been another vitally important factor behind Scotland retaining the most concentrated pattern of large-scale private land ownership in Europe.[6] Primogeniture was finally removed with respect to land through the Succession (Scotland) Act 1964, although it still survives for a range of titles, honours and dignities, including succession to the British throne.

Crucially, and despite the reforms of 1964, the inheritance of land still differs from other forms of property in that it is only with respect to land that spouses and issue have no right to a legal share. The Scottish Law Commission and others have proposed the removal of this anomaly since the 1960s.[7] These proposals were widely endorsed during formal consultations on them with the legal profession, civic groups and other interested parties. However, some landowning interests represented by the Scottish Landowners Federation and National Farmers Union were the notable exceptions to these endorsements and the issue remains to be resolved.

A special case for retaining the status quo can no longer be sustained on the argument that estates and other landed properties, while often wealthy in capital, are cash poor relative to other enterprises. Land owners also have the full range of fiscal opportunities to protect accumulated wealth as are available to everyone (e.g. trusts). Further there is no socio-economic or land use case for continuing to support artificially the survival of large landed properties. Many estates, while still representing a single unit of management, themselves already consist of several ownerships. There are other public and private arrangements available, rather than succession laws, to achieve necessary co-ordination in land management.

The Scottish Law Commission modified their proposals to try and reach a compromise with landowning interests.[8] They suggested that, for agricultural properties, there might be the option to pay spouses and issue their legal shares in annual instalments over ten years. However, there appears little justification for this in comparison to the equity of creating a level playing field with the same legal shares entitlement for all property. In any event, no progress was made.

Two other particular issues arise relative to succession. Firstly, the immortality of trusts and other corporate bodies. This can have a negative impact on the land market upon which the health of private property in a democracy depends. Secondly, in contrast to situations where immortality precludes succession, are the cases where there is no successor (when someone dies with no will and no known relations). In these latter cases, some pragmatic reform could be made to limit the lengths that have to be gone to under Scots law to determine whether there is indeed a successor. If no successor is traced, the property falls to the Crown. This reflects the basic principle in Scots law that everyone is related ('all Jock Tamson's bairns') and links back to the concept of the Crown representing the Community of the Realm.

Disposal

An authority to dispose of a title to land to someone else, whether by selling or gifting it, is one of the basic rights of land ownership. In contrast, tenants who can have rights of succession for their holdings similar to those of land owners and even a right to buy, can not by definition sell property they do not own.

This right of disposal is generally limited by other provisions (for example, that land can only be sold or gifted to persons entitled to hold it). However, under the current system of land tenure, there are also two particular intrusions on the right of disposal that can be conveyed by a seller in a title to land. These are *redemption* and *pre-emption*. Both these private rights exist to benefit the seller of land at the expense of the purchaser when that purchaser in turn wants to sell the land. The scope of each was significantly reduced by legislation in the 1970s (the Land Tenure Reform (Scotland) Act 1974). The replacement of the current feudal system of tenure provides an opportunity to complete their removal from land tenure altogether.

Rights of redemption date from the era when feudal superiors could have their cake and eat it. The right allows a former owner of land (usually the superior) to reacquire the land, either at their own discretion or at the occurrence of a specific event (for example, an heir coming of age). Normally, a price or at least a way of determining the price (for example, by arbitration) is specified. Rights of redemption reserved before 1974 still last in perpetuity, but the 1974 Act limited new reservations to a 20 year duration – the same limit that is put by law on particular types of long leases and is seen in Scots law as a period over which realistic expectations can be held (in comparison, for example, to a 99 year lease, where it is very much harder to predict changes that will have occurred in relevant factors by the end of the period) (see Chapter 14).

The reservation of rights of redemption has become relatively rare and it might be expected that, if they are not to be abolished altogether, then any perpetual reservations should be reduced to the 20 year duration and the creation of new reservations prohibited. Beyond arguments based on the fair operation of the land market, it can be argued that if someone wants to retain the level of interest represented by a right of redemption, then their appropriate legal mechanism is a lease.

Many of the same arguments are involved with a right of pre-emption – which requires an owner selling land to offer the property first to the person (usually the superior) to whom the right of pre-emption is reserved. This offer is usually at the price being offered by a prospective purchaser. The 1974 legislation reduced rights of pre-emption from a perpetual right to a once-only opportunity. It was also anticipated at that time that rights of pre-emption would subsequently be abolished, at least by prohibiting the reservation of new rights of pre-emption. This has not happened yet. There are, however, several instances of statutory rights to buy (for example, council houses and Scottish Office crofting estates) which overcome any existing pre-emption rights.

As the law currently stands, the 21-day offer period that the seller must allow to a potential pre-emptor, delays transactions and, if pre-emption is exercised, overrides the expenses and expectations of the prospective purchaser whose bid is being matched. It also potentially reduces the price obtained by the seller, compared to a situation where the pre-emptor might have competed in a fair and open market with everyone else. The fact that rights of pre-emption are exercised relatively infrequently, lends more support to their abolition than their retention.

It has been suggested that rights of pre-emption result in properties coming on the market that would not otherwise be sold.[9] An estate owner, for example, might be prepared to sell a redundant farm cottage because pre-emption would enable it to be reacquired at some point in the future, if it became needed again by the estate. However, there is no evidence that the 1974 reduction in rights of pre-emption had any effect on property sales and, as with redemption, a lease would be a more appropriate arrangement where an owner has genuine doubts about selling. Pre-emption is a historical mechanism that allows some land owners to hedge their bets at the expense of others. At present, rights of pre-emption are legally classified as a *land obligation*. This brings them within the jurisdiction of the Lands Tribunal for Scotland. This provides scope for the pre-emption to be varied or discharged, but this apparent flexibility does not of itself warrant the retention of these private rights within the system.

The main pretext for a right of pre-emption is not as at present as a private right, but as a public right exercised by government. This is common in European countries and allows the government to step in and purchase properties, under prescribed rules, where there is a warranted public interest.[10] This provides an option 'mid-way' between compulsory purchase and purchase by government on the open market. It might be construed in a theoretical sense that a right of pre-emption could already rest with the Crown or that, with the abolition of private rights of pre-emption, these fall to the Crown as a public right governed in its operation by Parliament from time to time.

There are a range of situations where the capacity of government to exercise a public right of pre-emption could be particularly useful. One example would be for land that has come to be seen as of national importance, for example, areas like the Cairngorms which the government has proposed should become National Parks. In such cases, there may be no compelling case for compulsory purchase yet too much is at stake for the public interest to run the chance of the open market, where a bid may not be successful.

This public right of pre-emption could also be linked to other new forms of intervention by the government in the land market in the public interest, whether to protect assets of national importance or because of particular local circumstances. One example would be to introduce arrangements that allowed proposed purchases of land in defined circumstances to be called in for consideration by the government and then, if approved, made subject to appropriate conditions (for example, the carrying out of an environmental audit or the production of a satisfactory management plan). This would be similar to the types of 'monopolies and merger' arrangements that already cover businesses. There might also be a case for provisions that enabled the government in defined circumstances to prevent sales for a set period to allow alternative bids of a certain character to be submitted. This would parallel existing provisions governing the sale of works of art of national importance that would otherwise be taken out of the country. In the land tenure context, the power might be a particularly valuable fallback on occasions to enable, for example, the position of a remote rural community to be safeguarded.

CHAPTER TWELVE

Arrangements for Shared and Common Ownership

This chapter considers the framework of options that exist within the land tenure system for owning land either individually or in shared ownership with others, including the different types of common land that can exist in Scotland.

Individual and Multiple Ownerships

All land in Scotland that has been granted out is in some form of shared ownership. At its simplest under the feudal system, the Crown and title holder are involved. Usually, the Crown, one or more superiors and the vassal in possession of the land are involved. This pattern can be seen as the traditional feudal pyramid, with a number of different owners all having an interest in the same land. However, as particular owners can be superiors and vassals in different situations, the pattern can be a complex web. This is further complicated, as some specific rights in land can be held and conveyed separately from the land itself (for example, mineral rights).

Under a reformed system of land tenure, this pattern would be simplified. All titles to land would be held by entitled persons (natural and legal) directly under the Crown. There would be no intervening superiors. The scope to separate out and convey particular rights like mineral and salmon fishing rights might also be reduced and rationalised (see Chapter 13).

Within this reformed pattern, entitled persons would still be able to hold a title to land either individually or with other entitled persons. However, as part of the reforms, there is the opportunity to clarify what constitutes an individually held or single ownership and the framework of different types of shared ownerships that can exist between entitled persons over the same land, including the essential features of the relationships between those persons in each situation.

Single Ownership

Land can be described as individually held and having a single owner where there is only one title to that land and that title is vested in one named person (natural or legal). This position has to be qualified, however, by defining the number of people that can be involved even when a title conveys land to one named person.

(i) A Natural Person

A single named natural person represents more than one individual when that person is married. Legislation has granted spouses legal rights over matrimonial homes that almost amount to those of a co-owner, despite the fact that a spouse may not be named on the title deed. This applies equally whether the named person is the only named owner or one of a number of co-owners. Co-ownership by spouses is now a well established principle in law and one where, in its implementation, there will be a continuing need to leave adequate discretion to the courts to deal with particular circumstances (for example, exclusion orders for violent spouses). However, there will also be an ongoing requirement to refine the legislative framework.

This refinement needs to include relatively technical issues, such as clarification of the rights of an un-named spouse against the rights of other named co-owners. However, broader issues will also be involved. Matrimonial homes have, for example, already been broadly defined by the legislation, but how far should an un-named spouse's rights of co-ownership extend over any associated land and other property rights held by the named spouse? This issue marks the transition from the origins of the matrimonial homes legislation as a response to hardship cases, to wider issues of social justice associated with the property of spouses (for example, see Chapter 11).

Over and above the question of extending the entitlement principle from homes to land more generally, is the wider issue still of the status attributed to a marriage contract as traditionally defined. In Scotland, and the UK as a whole, marriage is becoming an increasingly transitory relationship (current figures indicate over 50% separation/divorce rates) and a declining proportion of co-habitants and parents are becoming married at all, therefore placing greater reliance on adequate definitions in Scots law of common law husbands and wives.

(ii) A Legal Person

A single named legal person as title holder or land owner can represent very many people (for example, the shareholders of a company named as title holder). However, this is still a single ownership as only one named owner and one legal interest is involved (i.e. the company).

The one exception to this is where the single named legal person is a trust or unincorporated association (for example, a club). This has been classified as joint ownership because the trustees or members are considered the owners, rather than the trust or association itself. However, individual trustees or members have no separate or separable rights of ownership (for example, the capacity to sell their share) and the trust or club has to act as a single entity.

This situation is really a product of the constitution of the title holder, rather than any genuine issue of multiple ownership. There is a need to decide more clearly whether trusts and unincorporated associations have sufficient legal identity to act as title holders. If they do, then they should be capable of being treated as conventional single owners. If they do not, they would need to reconstitute themselves if they wished to own property. Either answer would resolve the ambiguities currently associated with the transfer of property by these types of bodies.[1]

There are potentially other reasons for excluding private trusts from land ownership (for example, lack of transparency over their beneficiaries, see Chapter 11). They might have to become, for example, publicly accountable companies or charities. However, if trusts were given a clearer legal identity as owners in their own right, this would be as a single owner. In England, trust ownership is considered divided (i.e. shared) between the trustees and beneficiary. However, in Scotland, trust ownership is considered full and undivided. The right of beneficiaries is only a personal right to require implementation of the trust's purposes.

Resolving the issue of trust and association ownership would largely eliminate the category of 'joint property'. At the same time, the only other instance of it might also be discontinued, thus completing the removal of 'joint property' from Scots land law. This involves cases where joint ownership has been intentionally created by the terms in which a title is conveyed to two or more persons. It appears most legal authorities consider that it is already no longer possible to do this.[2]

It is not apparent that there are any reasons that warrant persons who are joint owners, whether by choice or not, having less rights as owners than other persons who share the ownership of land. Joint ownership could be converted into shared ownership by giving existing joint owners the same basic rights of other co-owners (see below).

Shared Ownership

Shared ownership exists where two or more persons hold titles to the same individual property. It is a single ownership in the practical sense that the property (land) is an undivided whole. However, it is shared ownership in the legal reality that each of the owners involved can bequeath, sell or burden their share separately.

The land involved in shared property is labelled *common property* in the existing system of land tenure, because it is an undivided whole held by several owners. This label did not become standard practice until the mid 19th century, by which time more genuine forms of common property (such as village greens and burgh commons) had already become largely extinct (see Chapter 12).[3] The current legal framework governing shared property might be considered to reflect a now unreasonable 19th century bias against common property.[4] The key feature of this is the authority invested in each individual co-owner against the co-owners as a collective interest (for example, the power of one to force a division of the common property).

For practical purposes, common property can be considered in two main categories. Firstly, co-ownership as covered in this sub-section, involving straightforward shared ownership of a particular property between two or more persons with considerable flexibility to divide the property between them. Secondly, common ownership as covered under the next sub-heading, involving properties that are held in common between owners as a result of their title to *other* exclusively held land and where there can be significantly less scope to divide the common property.

There is considerable scope to make the current legal framework governing conventional shared ownership more up-to-date, more straightforward and fairer. There are two main requirements. Firstly, there is a need to maintain a high level of flexibility in the possible arrangements between co-owners, including in matters dealing with the division of the property. Secondly, it is important to balance measures to ensure adequate security and fair rights of use for all the co-owners against the rights given to each individual co-owner. Part of this would involve tempering the near absolute right in most forms of shared property of individual co-owners to force a division of the whole property. At the same time, the unlimited right of a co-owner to sub-divide their share of co-owned property without necessary reason, should be placed within fair limits to safeguard the interests of other co-owners.

The general presumption that shares are equal unless specified should be maintained, while the options for mathematical shares are reduced. Also, any legal scope that might be considered to exist for majority voting should be removed. The circumstances that are not limited by the principle of consensus could be elaborated, including protection (for example, driving off deer even against the wishes of other co-owners) and necessary repairs (for example, repairing a leaking roof with a right to recompense from co-owners).

There are already some recognised principles covering fair use. These include the right of each co-owner to use all the shared property for 'ordinary' uses, so that other co-owners can do the same and not allowing excessive benefit to one owner (for example, using a common hallway for access but not for storage). The flexibility for co-owners to reach contractual agreements over the management of the whole property should be maintained, but only as a personal contract not binding on successors.

Shared ownership is largely governed at present by a number of disparate legal decisions from cases scattered across recent centuries. There is considerable opportunity, as with other aspects of land tenure, for a review of shared ownership to produce a relatively straightforward or codified set of governing principles.

Common Ownership

Within the broad sphere of shared ownership, a number of special forms of co-ownership exist to address particular situations. The arrangements for matrimonial homes, for example, are a very specific case based in the first instance on the relationship between the co-owners.

A principal category of co-ownership is determined by the character of the land involved and results in several forms of common ownership. In these cases, either the natural character of the land or some special feature of its legal nature, makes it inherently unsuitable for division between the co-owners. A further basic feature of common ownership in this sense, is that the land involved is held as an extension of, or appendage to, other exclusively held property. Thus, each co-owner's stake in the common property only derives from their ownership of other land. In each different type of case, specific legal rules are required to govern the relationship between the co-owners for that type of common property.

The most widespread type of common property is that associated with tenement buildings. Owners who hold parts of the building exclusively (for example, as flats) may, by virtue of that ownership, have a share in the undivided common ownership of other parts of the building (for example, the stairs). In these cases, while owners are free to bequeath or sell their exclusively owned property and thus a share in the common property, the indispensable nature of the common property generally makes its division impractical. In such instances, the co-owners have an equal share in the common property independent of the size of the exclusively owned property through which they derive their share. This rule also applies to another relatively extensive form of common property – freshwater lochs that are not entirely enclosed within a single ownership.

The status of these lochs as common property is, of course, not due to their indispensable nature to the surrounding owners but to the sheer impracticality of division in most instances. The owners, whatever the size of their frontage to the loch, own from that frontage up to some theoretical mid point with the other co-owners, but in reality have rights over the whole loch. The legal rules in relation to these common property lochs are, however, out of date and need systematic review to bring them into line with modern uses and capabilities. The Scottish Law Commission has already made proposals for updating the laws of tenement and further proposals are anticipated soon.[5]

A third form of common property is commonties (and the closely related scattalds under udal tenure in Shetland). Historically, commonties were the most extensive form of undivided common private property in Scotland. Their operation and socio-economic importance, together with their relatively rapid conversion into exclusively held private property during the 18th and 19th centuries, are described in detail in *A Pattern of Landownership in Scotland*. That book also shows that, while some legal authorities may wonder whether there are any commonties left, there are strong indications that a number of commonties (and scattalds) still survive in the Scottish countryside.[6]

Commonties are not distinguished by the type of land involved, although usually they were relatively extensive upland areas. Their widespread division reflects that there were essentially no practical difficulties in physically splitting them up between the different owners. The 1695 Act of the old Scots Parliament for the division of commonties provided a relatively quick and easy legal mechanism for carrying this out. That Act is still in force.

Commonties constituted a distinct form of land holding or tenure, with rights of ownership in a commonty based on the ownership of neighbouring (but not necessarily adjoining) land. While sometimes just associated with a particular group of properties, they were also often associated with all the separately owned properties in a parish. The commonty resources shared between all the land owners in a parish were thus also available to all the land owners' tenants and so a shared resource between all the inhabitants of the parish.

For commonties that have survived into the current era, the terms of the 1695 Act should be considered no longer appropriate. The authority given by that Act for one party to force the division of a commonty should be replaced by a more balanced and flexible approach. More generally than that, commonties might be considered a distinctive form of tenure that could once again play a valuable part in Scotland's system of land tenure. The 1695 Act could be repealed and commonties re-constituted in contemporary terms by fresh legislation. These commonties would have two principal advantages as a distinct form of shared private property. Firstly, security, as they would not be vulnerable to the strong presumption in favour of division usually associated with co-ownership. Secondly, clarity, as their operation would be governed universally by clear legal rules, in comparison to the uncertainty associated with the usual wide discretion of operation with most other forms of co-ownership.

The potential for newly constituted commonties might be considered to span the whole landscape, from urban street corners to remote mountain tops. With the former, examples might include a development in which several individually held properties (for example, houses and business premises) also held and managed an area of land in common (for example, amenity parkland or woodland). The latter, remoter instances might be seen as a reversal of an earlier historic trend. In the 18th and 19th centuries, many commonties disappeared when all the properties that had had a share came into a single ownership. Nowadays, as the largest estates tend to be broken up into a number of smaller estates, it might be advantageous to have an arrangement whereby the ownership of extensive upland areas can again be shared in common between a number of neighbouring properties. Commonties could also offer a useful form of tenure for community based ownership. This includes their potential to be managed as a whole through a lease to a third party controlled by the co-owners.

Commonties are not the only distinct form of common property to have survived in Scotland and more examples of different types (for example, common peat mosses and resting stances at river crossings) are likely to come to light as comprehensive land registration gradually fills in the map of who owns what.[7] As part of reforming land tenure, there is scope to review each of these types and if warranted, establish a modern set of arrangements.

A review of that nature would need to be fully integrated with consideration of the closely related legal framework of common interests that can exist between different owners (see following chapter). In the past, there has often been considerable difficulty distinguishing whether the rights involved in particular areas have been ones of common use or common ownership.[8]

CHAPTER THIRTEEN

The Relationships Between Different Owners

Rights and Interests

Chapter 12 described the legal relationships that can exist between owners where they are co-owners of the same land. This section describes the relationships between the owners of different properties. These properties would normally be those of neighbours or near neighbours but, under Scotland's feudal system, these different properties can also be the same land. The interests of superiors (*dominium directum*) constitute separate ownerships that overlap their vassals' ownerships (*dominium utile*). Many different aspects still survive to the legal relationships that can exist between superiors and vassals as a consequence of their respective, overlapping ownerships.

There has been a long-standing historical trend to reduce the influence a superior can have over a vassal and the vassal's land. The abolition of superiorities would finally sweep away the remnants of this complex and archaic pattern. However, this move needs to be linked to a more wide-ranging review of what might be considered the legitimate relationships that can exist between different owners by virtue of their different ownerships. What influence, for example, is it reasonable in different situations that one land owner should be able to exert over another owner's use of that other owner's land?

There are several clear components required in a framework of such relationships. There are, for example, the many instances where neighbouring land owners share *common interests* (for example, a boundary wall) and also where owners have *rights of servitude* over the lands of other owners for practical reasons (for example, access to a water supply). There are also the types of rights that owners require to give them reasonable protection from the actions of other owners (for example, *encroachment* and *nuisance*). Beyond these 'natural justice' aspects, there is the issue of the extent to which one owner should be able to impose *obligations* and *conditions* (akin to the private regulation of vassals by superiors) on the land of other owners.

These types of relationships between the owners of different lands are considered below. However, there is also, in addition to superiorities, one other category of overlapping ownership that needs to be addressed – *separate tenements*. This legal label refers to certain components of land (for example, minerals) and particular rights over it (for example, salmon fishing) that can be owned separately from the land itself.

As such, separate tenements carry the normal basic rights of ownership and can, for example, be bequeathed, sold and leased independently of the ownership of the land of which they form a part. The normal types of relationship that can exist between different owners also apply (for example, common interest). However, the physical intimacy of the relationship with separate tenements means that there can also be particular consequences for the relationship between the owners involved, for example, for a house owner when the owner of the mineral rights wishes to exploit these. The position of separate tenements will not be affected by the abolition of superiorities. However, separate tenements are also of feudal origin[1] and the status of each of the main different types of separate tenement needs to be reviewed.

Separate Tenements

The general principle of land ownership in Scotland is that the owner of the surface of land (known as *the solum*) owns everything – all the heritable property from the heavens to the centre of the earth (*'a coelo usque ad centrum'*). Separate tenements (defined above) go against this principle and they have only been recognised in Scots land law to a limited extent. They are legally unsatisfactory as an intrusion into what is considered the natural integrity of ownership. They can also be a particular source of legal disputes when, in this unusual juxtapositioning of ownerships, different owners are trying to exercise their separate rights in the same place.

Separate tenements can also be illogical from the point of view of satisfactory natural resource management. The right to fish for salmon, for example, can be owned by one person who has no right of management or control over the water in which their right might be exercised; that management and control remains with the riparian owner, who may have no right to fish for salmon. In addition, it can be argued that the separation of certain rights of ownership from the solum can have adverse socio-economic consequences (see below). These can relate not just to the disadvantages for the owner of the solum, but also more generally to the locality where the solum is situated.

The reform of land tenure in Scotland provides an opportunity to rationalise and reduce the scope for separate tenements. The outcome of such a review can be anticipated to vary for different types of separate tenements. While there has been a legalistic tendency to group them according to conveyancing procedure,[2] they can be considered in this context as consisting of three main types.

One type derives from the rights of the Crown in all land and consists of the Crown rights legally capable of being granted out as separate property rights or ownerships, for example, rights over the foreshore. The existence of this type of separate tenement is of medieval origin and reflects particular assets and rights over which the Crown wanted to retain control because of their significance at that time. The Crown making such reservations was not unusual in itself. The Crown will continue to have rights in all land in a reformed system of land tenure for Scotland. What was exceptional, even in terms of Scots legal theory at the time and since, was that some of these became conveyable as separate ownerships (e.g. mineral rights). It might have been expected that, as in most other countries, the rights which became granted out would have attached straightforwardly to the ownership of the land itself or solum.[3]

The scope at present to review these Crown-derived separate tenements is illustrated by the continuing confusion over the full range of rights that can be involved. Then, amongst the rights that might be recognised, some have become irrelevant through the passage of time and others have been overtaken by statutory regulation. With the remainder, it might be considered that some should be no longer granted out as separate rights from the land to which they pertain, while it can also be questioned whether some others should still be granted out into private ownership at all.

The existing separate tenements that are either Crown rights or derived from them are covered in Section 3 above, together with the rights more generally that the Crown has in all land. These latter rights stem from the Crown's position as the source of 'ownership', rather than 'an owner'. They do not constitute separate tenements. Beyond this, in a reformed system of land tenure, it might be considered that Crown rights should no longer be a source of separate tenements.

The other two types of separate tenements do not derive directly from Crown rights and thus only involve private rights. They occur in two distinct circumstances: ownerships above and below the solum or surface of the land.

The former only involve buildings (for example, flats or tenements in the conventional Scottish use of the word). An extensive body of legal rules has evolved from the 19th century to govern the relationship between the different owners in tenement situations. These rules (known as the *law of the tenement*) have not kept pace with the times in a number of respects (for example, rights and responsibilities for carrying out repairs). They need to be reviewed to bring them up to date so that they are both pragmatic and fair. This is something the Scottish Law Commission has already reported on and on which it is due to report again in the near future with further proposals for reforms.[4]

The recognition of separate tenements in buildings is an ongoing practical requirement, reflecting the reality of settlement patterns in Scotland (and most other countries). There is nothing particularly exceptional about this and this type of separate tenement barely constitutes a separate tenement in a traditional sense. The intrusion of one ownership into another is, for example, largely theoretical. The ownerships, rather than trying to share the same actual space, are essentially stacked vertically above and below each other in a reasonably distinct fashion (from the point of view of distinguishing ownership, even if not architecturally!).

The third and final type of separate tenement only involves the ownership of minerals. There have been attempts by land owners to establish some other rights as separate tenements. The most notable is hunting rights, where the position has been progressively eroded to the extent that there is a need to re-establish beyond doubt that hunting rights can not be conveyed separately.[5] To allow hunting rights as a separate tenement would be bad for sound land use and against local socio-economic interests. It would also breach the well established legal principle that the separate tenements which do not derive directly from Crown rights should only involve corporeal property (the thing itself) rather than incorporeal property (a right to a thing).

To be in line with this principle, a separate tenement of minerals is not just a right of mining in Scotland's current land tenure arrangements. It is construed as the ownership of the underground geological strata. Thus, in contrast to the above ground law of tenement, a separate tenement of minerals is a considerable intrusion into the principle of the integrity of ownership. It can become the dominant interest in any land. The exploitation of minerals can result in destruction of the existing surface of the land (with the owner of the surface possibly only compensated for the physical damage).

In that physical and practical sense, minerals as a separate tenement can be considered as a negation of the principle of land ownership. Its status can also be seen as something of an aberration even within the context of separate tenements. It arose during the medieval era by extending the Crown's reservation of certain minerals (for example, gold and silver) to cover all the other unreserved minerals for the benefit of private land owners.

There are some issues to be resolved about the interface between the minerals reserved to the Crown and those that can be held as separate private tenements. There are also more extensive issues to sort out related to the conveyancing of mineral rights, such as whether all non-Crown mineral rights are automatically covered however long ago the separate tenement was established and more or less independently of the terms in which it was then granted.

These and related mineral issues are discussed further in Chapters 5 and 14. The distinction between ownership and rights of use could, as in most countries, be more clearly established. The separation of ownership and minerals could be restricted, for example, only to defined timespan leases of rights of use. This would safeguard the rights of land ownership and resolve many of the issues associated with specifying what minerals might be involved. It would also be likely to confer environmental and socio-economic benefits, while reducing disputes (see Chapter 9).

Burdens and Conditions

Scotland's system of land tenure is exceptional for the extent of rights and interests, over and above any separate tenements, that one land owner can have in the land of another owner.

These rights and interests, while they can not be conveyed separately, are still property rights or rights of a proprietary character as they are dependent on the ownership of land. The two (or more) different ownerships involved have traditional legal labels. The ownership in whose favour they operate is the *dominant tenement* (or property) and the ownership subject to them is the *servient tenement*. Legislation (1970) has put it another way, labelling them the *benefited* and *burdened* ownerships.

The range of these reciprocal rights and obligations that can still exist between different owners in Scotland is particularly complex, not least as a result of Scotland's feudal history. The different types of interests that can be involved, which can be classified in various ways, are grouped into two main sets here.

The need for one of these main sets of rights is relatively straightforward. Neighbouring land owners have always interacted over their respective ownerships and, over the centuries, a set of related legal rules has evolved to provide a framework for regulating these interactions fairly. These different types of rights and interests, which cover for example the laws of common interests and nuisance, are often collectively labelled the *law of neighbourhood* (see below). Importantly, these rights and interests between owners are enjoyed by all land owners and are essentially not dependent on the terms of their title deeds.

This sub-section considers the second main set of rights and interests – those that one land owner can have in the land of another owner by virtue of burdens and conditions inserted in that other owner's title deed. These burdens and conditions are most clearly a legacy of feudalism in Scotland. The essence of feudal tenure is as a conditional system. The superior grants the vassal land subject to the vassal fulfilling various obligations. Originally, these involved providing support with a set number of armed men when called for, as well as providing other goods and services for the superior's household. Many of these characteristic burdens and conditions of ancient feudalism have disappeared as a result of reforms, notably the Heritable Jurisdictions (Scotland) Act 1746 and Feudal Casualties (Scotland) Act 1914.

The remaining scope to impose burdens and conditions, while still very extensive, is not now generally seen as feudal, as the types of burdens and conditions allowed can be imposed independent of a feudal grant. They can be established in any outright grant (i.e. where no new superiority is created) as long as the granter retains the ownership of a property to which the burdens and conditions can be related. Thus, while the separate ownership can be a superiority, it need not be.

On this basis, these burdens and conditions need not be unduly affected by the abolition of feudal tenure in Scotland. There would perhaps be some slight reduction in their scope. This is because the intimate nature of a superior's interest in their vassal's land means they can, in theory at least, more readily impose constraints on the use of that land.[6] However, it has been suggested that existing superiors' interests could be fairly readily carried straight across as *land conditions* into a new, non-feudal system of land tenure.[7]

The position of monetary burdens might be seen as an exception to this. Firstly, the scope for recurrent payments could be swept away. The need to finally abolish feu duties is well established, but a range of other archaic perpetual charges could similarly be extinguished (for example, multures associated with mills, and tiends and stipends, originally involving payments to support the local minister). Secondly, land should no longer be burdened with capital payments. The use of land as security for loans/debts should only be a personal contract between the parties involved. Also, these arrangements should be essentially of only one type. Building on existing provisions, they should all have to follow the form defined for *standard securities*. There might also be a case for reviewing the validity of allowing non-monetary conditions. The very concept of these breaches the basic presumption in Scots law that the ownership of land should be free from perpetual burdens.[8]

This presumption is, in part, reflected in the requirement that any condition that is to *run with the land* (i.e. affect successive owners) should be clearly stated in title deeds. This can place great emphasis on the particular wording and nuances in title deeds, as the courts are generally unsympathetic to what might have been intended or what might be implied. However, beyond this, there is almost unlimited scope to impose any lawful restriction, so long as it can be seen to regulate the use of the servient property for the benefit of the dominant ownership (rather than its owner for the time being). Examples of these conditions are given below.

The benefit involved can also be very limited. While owners, superiors and other equivalent title holders, have to have *title and interest* to be able to enforce such conditions, the possession of a title is generally considered a sufficient interest. The only exception is related to the opportunities that exist for co-feuars and other owners subject to the same shared conditions, to enforce them against each other. In these cases, some more genuine or financial interest has to be demonstrated.

This system of private regulation, whereby one owner can intrude into the use and enjoyment of another owner's land, first emerged in the late 18th century. Its consolidation as part of Scots land law is particularly associated with the development of Edinburgh's New Town during the late 18th and early 19th centuries. Typical obligations imposed nowadays include requirements to build to a particular plan or to refrain from building, to maintain land or buildings in a particular condition (for example, the colour of paint on window frames) or to refrain from particular uses of the land and buildings (for example, not keeping pets or carrying on any trade or business).

While the power to impose such conditions can be seen historically to have brought benefits to developments such as Edinburgh's New Town, it is no longer clear what the justification for such a system is now. It tends to be only justified on the grounds of historical benefits and its continuance excused by the ability, since 1979, to have unreasonable, inappropriate or unduly burdensome conditions varied or removed by applying to the Lands Tribunal for Scotland. The Tribunal could be made more accessible in this role, but wider reforms are required.

Many aspects that can be covered by this private regulation

should now only be dealt with under existing statutory provisions, such as the planning system or environmental health legislation. Why should some owners have to get special permission, often at significant cost, from one owner in addition to going through an extensively developed statutory planning system? Beyond that, the switch should be made from one owner having controls over the activities of many other owners, to each owner being able to defend themselves and their interests against the actions of other owners. This can be secured through the law of neighbourhood (see below). This would ensure that the interests involved are genuine and fair.

Particular arrangements should also be instigated to deal with situations currently covered by Deeds of Conditions. These are most common in housing developments, where a developer imposes standard conditions on all those acquiring houses in the development. The individual title deeds simply refer to the single Deed of Conditions, to avoid repetition of all the conditions in each title. To the extent that any arrangement over and above the law of neighbourhood is required, the arrangement should be one between, and under the equitable control of, the participants. They should not be governed by the interests of an unaccountable third party.

In future, the only land conditions by one owner on another owner which are not related to the law of neighbourhood, should be restricted to personal contracts that do not run with the land. This would remove these land conditions (a unique form of personal contract at present because they carry over to successors [9]) from title deeds and the Land Register and integrate them more generally into the Scots law of obligations.

This would also link them into other types of legitimate contracts over land (for example, the contracts signed between the Forestry Commission and land owners when the Forestry Commission gives the owner a grant to manage or expand woodlands). Such contracts might be viewed as 'fittings' associated with the land but not a compulsory component acquired with the land, as against the current conditions which can be regarded as permanent 'fixtures'. The boundary to the extent of acceptable contracts, in terms of the control they grant over land, might be defined by what is determined to constitute a lease (see Chapter 14).

Neighbourhood Laws

A number of rights and interests exist by which land owners can defend the practical use and peaceful enjoyment of their property from actions (or the lack of them) by neighbouring land owners.

These rights and interests, like the burdens and conditions described above, operate between different ownerships and their enforcement by one owner against another is dependent on an appropriate title deed. However, unlike burdens and conditions, these rights and interests can be enjoyed by all land owners essentially independent of the terms of their title. They exist to regulate the interactions between the lands of different owners through rules of acceptable behaviour. They are based in the common law of Scotland – reflecting their ancient origins. They have mainly evolved through legal precedents from court decisions, but have also become increasingly influenced by statutory provisions.

While the rights and interests involved are sometimes labelled as the law of neighbourhood, this is not a clearly defined set of laws or area of law. However, there is considerable scope to consolidate and develop it, as part of moving away from the imposition by some owners of burdens and conditions on other owners, towards each and every owner having equitable rights of self-defence against the actions of other owners.

The law of neighbourhood could be clarified by listing and defining the types of rights and interests attributed to land owners through it. The outcome of a systematic review could be seen as part of a wider 'civil code' of the rights and responsibilities that are attached to the ownership of land independent of a particular title to land.

At the heart of these responsibilities is the existing duty to have reasonable regard to the interests of other owners and people more generally (for example, safety).[10] While this duty is based on ownership, it needs to be clear that it resides with and is incumbent on the owner(s). The land owner is only relieved of that duty to the extent that someone else is legitimately in occupation of the land or has control over its use (for example, a tenant).

Owners' rights of defence against the actions of other owners are mainly based on the laws of nuisance and negligence generally.

However, a number of other groups of rights are also involved. Two such groups from land law are considered here before further consideration of the law of nuisance.

(i) Servitudes

Servitudes appear closely related to burdens and conditions because they give one land owner the right to use another owner's land for a particular purpose. However, servitudes are differently constituted.[11] They can be seen as a pragmatic arrangement to govern the relationship between properties where one is dependent on the other in some reasonable and practical way (for example, a right of access or to make use of a water supply).

It is in the nature of servitudes that they must place no requirement on the servient ownership to do anything, except to refrain from interfering with the legitimate exercise of the servitude. At the same time, that operation must be carried out 'courteously' in its broadest sense. The established use can not be significantly altered and must only be for the practical benefit of the dominant ownership. Resources obtained can not, for example, be sold nor the right given to any third party. The benefit can also not be a personal benefit to the owner (for example, a sporting right can not be a servitude).

While servitudes do not have to appear in titles, they should only 'run with the land', ruling out the one possible category at present of personal servitudes (*liferent* or the personal use for life of another's property).[12] Servitudes should also only be positive rights, ruling out the only negative one recognised at present – against building on the servient property that prevents light reaching the dominant ownership. This is a matter that should be dealt with elsewhere (for example, planning legislation), just as some other concerns are (for example, rights of privacy). Thus, servitudes would only be categorised by the practical benefit they confer in relation to buildings (for example, the right in a tenement building to insert a beam) or land (for example, the right to a water supply).

Historically, the interpretation of the nuances of feudal titles was often of significance in determining whether rights of servitude, as opposed to common property, existed. This was particularly the case during the main period when commonties were being divided. Some of these types of complex patterns of rights still survive in the contemporary Scottish countryside (see Chapter 12).[13]

There is scope for servitudes to cover a wide range of natural resource uses (for example, grazing livestock, cutting peat or self-sown timber, collecting seaweed or other natural produce, erecting a weir across a river to lead water to a mill). While some authors have tried to list these uses,[14] it is a well established principle that the types of servitude possible should always be open ended to meet changing circumstances. Similarly, there is scope for servitudes over particular natural resource uses to be shared between several owner-ships (for example, all the property owners in a village or parish sharing the grazing rights over an area of hill that belongs to a single owner).

The flexibility of servitudes needs to be maintained as a broad category of rights by which owners can safeguard the use and enjoy-ment of their property. However, servitudes should also be a tightly controlled category of rights. There should continue to be a general presumption against them as an intrusion into the ownership of another. Servitudes already come within the jurisdiction of the Lands Tribunal for Scotland and, by making the Tribunal's proce-dures more generally accessible, safeguards over servitudes could be improved.

Servitudes can be seen as serving the practical utilities of the benefited ownership and, in a reformed system of land tenure, they could be more closely linked to related statutory provisions associ-ated with public utilities. These include powers to lay pipes, cables etc. across land and are often labelled as statutory wayleaves. The rights involved are not between different ownerships, but in other respects resemble those associated with servitudes.[15]

(ii) Common Interests

A second type of right of practical importance to land owners in the defence of the use and enjoyment of their property, is where a common interest is shared with one or more other ownerships.

As a type of right, common interest has a number of similarities with servitudes. It is between ownerships (not owners directly) and only occurs between neighbouring (but not necessarily contiguous) ownerships. It is a practical right that does not appear in title deeds and is only regulated by law and equity.[16] Common interest can involve one owner restraining the actions of another (for example, from knocking down a supporting wall in a shared building). However, common interest, in comparison to servitudes, can involve one owner requiring another to take positive actions on the other's property (for example, to maintain a supporting wall).

The main sphere with which common interest is associated is tenement buildings, as the close proximity of ownerships means that the activities of one owner can often affect (materially or substantially) the interests of others. The rules involved warrant rationalisation as part of wider reforms of the law of tenement. However, as with servitudes, there are advantages in not defining them too closely so as to retain sufficient flexibility to regulate fairly the common interests of neighbouring proprietors.

There is also a current need to establish more clearly the situations other than tenement buildings where common interest can apply and the rules under which it operates in different circumstances. With tenement buildings, these rules, including the grounds for enforcement, generally involve pragmatic aspects such as safety, stability or servicing common areas. However, with other types of common interest, the rules have been more broadly related to the amenity and enjoyment of property.

One of these specific areas of common interest are the marches or boundaries between properties, where the properties adjoin directly (for example, with no common property between them). Thus, proprietors may each own to the mid point of a boundary wall, while having a common interest in the whole wall. Parts of this aspect of common interest are still covered by the 1661 March Dykes Act of the Scots Parliament, but modernisation is required.[17]

A related common interest can exist over the full width of a river, where the boundary between properties is down the middle of the river. The owners of a loch in shared ownership also have a common interest in the management of the loch as a whole. Importantly, in the case of a stream or river, all the ownerships through which it passes are considered to have a common interest in the water as a whole. This means that any of these riparian owners are limited in their use of the river by the interests of all the other riparian owners.

It appears that the nature of these common interest rights in water has not been fully explored for the potential scope of their implications for common resource management (for example, to ensure high environmental standards of use by other owners). The opportunities to establish common interest rights between owners in other environmental resources might also be explored (for example, types of wildlife, like deer, that move between properties).

(iii) Nuisance

In Scots law, nuisance is a narrower and more distinct legal category of rights and interests between different owners than the equivalent area of English law. In Scotland, the law of nuisance is not directly involved in the regulation of common interests, servitudes, the law of tenement or other aspects of law dealing with the relationships between owners, such as encroachment, malicious action and negligence.[18]

Within Scotland's law of neighbourhood, nuisance can be considered as providing a final set of broad principles and legal rules to resolve the conflicting interests of neighbours, where other remedies do not address the issue. Thus, for example, if negligence can be established then there will be no need to have recourse to the law of nuisance.

Essentially, nuisance can be defined as an intolerable interference with the use and enjoyment of an owner's land (for example, due to noise or smell).[19] There are two distinct elements – the nuisance itself (action/effect) and liability. However, while it is now established in Scots law that blame needs to be shown rather than the mere existence of harm, the onus on the complainer to prove liability is in fairness reasonably limited.

The key thing for the complainer to demonstrate is *material* harm. This need not be material in a physical sense and is broadly interpreted to encompass, for example, discomfort and inconvenience. Aspects such as standards of public morality can be invoked, but the complainer's personal tastes or sensitivities are not relevant. Nuisance is determined on the basis of what 'a reasonable person' should not be required to tolerate. The fact that the complainer may have known about the activity constituting the nuisance before acquiring the property does not constrain the right to complain, nor does he or she have to tolerate the nuisance if, for example, the activity can be construed to be in the national interest.

Nuisance is usually associated with causes such as noise, vibration, fumes and other forms of pollution. However, the sources are unlimited in law and factors such as the nature of a locality or the time of day an activity occurs, can all be influential in determining nuisance. Each case involves questions of circumstances, fact and degree and the courts recognise that a balancing process can be involved, with a need to take account of the interests of both parties.

Something of that balancing process underpins the law of neighbourhood as a whole – providing each owner with rights and interests to defend the use and enjoyment of their land, while at the same time imposing responsibilities and duties on all land owners to act reasonably so as not to interfere unduly with their neighbours.

Nuisance is only one component of the law of neighbourhood, but the broadness and flexibility of its application make it the essence of that sector of law. As with the other components, there is scope to review and consolidate the law of nuisance as part of establishing a revised law of neighbourhood (one free of one-sided burdens and conditions, incorporating a more straightforward law of tenement and so on, as discussed above). Such a review of nuisance would be likely to re-establish the coherent and distinct identity of nuisance in Scots law, after the uncertainty deriving from the influence of English law in recent decades in particular.

The law of nuisance is based in the common law of Scotland. Its modern development dates from the second half of the 18th century and more especially the 19th century. In very large measure, its emergence was a response to the industrial revolution and public health movements. At that time, nuisance and closely related aspects of common law played an early and important role in environmental protection by providing grounds for action against polluters.

Nowadays, this type of private regulation has very largely been replaced by parliamentary measures which provide a statutory basis for the control of pollution and other environmental and social standards. These measures have clearly produced huge benefits. However, in some instances, the setting of statutory standards can be considered to have legitimised certain levels of pollution and environmental damage and to have thus lowered standards from those that might have been pursued successfully under common law (for example, water quality).[20]

This observation does not discount or undervalue the need for the statutory measures. However, the understandable focus in the growth of environmental legislation on measures to control the actions that owners can carry out on their own land, has partially obscured the question of what continuing or newly created roles property rights can have "in the defence of nature".[21] On one hand, the acquisition of land or other property rights to achieve conservation objectives in the particular situations is well recognised, for example, buying land to establish a nature reserve or buying out certain rights, such as shooting rights, to protect particular species.[22] However, on the other hand, the scope to use property related rights to regulate the anti-social behaviour or actions of other owners (for example, over the flow or water quality of a river) still warrants further examination.

CHAPTER FOURTEEN

The Leasing of Land

Owners and tenants are the two types of statutory occupiers of land in Scotland. This chapter describes the rights of owners to lease their land to tenants and the different forms of tenancies in Scots law. Consideration is also given to other types of contractual arrangements that can exist over land but which do not constitute leases.

Lease Holders

In Scots law, only land (immoveable property) can be the subject of a lease (the equivalent arrangement for moveable property is defined as hire). A lease is a contract by which someone (*the tenant*) is allowed to occupy someone else's property (*the landlord's*) for a finite term (*duration*) in return for periodic payments (*rent*). Generally, the tenant has exclusive occupation; otherwise, if the occupation is shared with the landlord, the right is one of *licence* rather than lease. However, hunting, salmon fishing and mineral leases are notable exceptions to this (see below).

The authority of owners to grant leases over all or part of their property is considered one of the basic rights of land ownership.[1] It is an authority that has been exercised very extensively throughout the history of land ownership in Scotland. Legislation safeguarding the rights of tenants is amongst the oldest extant Acts in Scots law (namely, the Leases Act 1449).

As leases are contracts, some of the many rules governing them are the subject of contract law. However, the law of leases has always been a substantial sector of the legal system of land tenure in Scotland. The near matching size of the 'paired volumes' produced by some authors on the laws of ownership and leases,[2] is also an indication of the extent to which they deal with a similar range of topics, albeit from the different points of view of an owner and a tenant.

Within land tenure in Scotland, tenancy can be considered as the third level of occupation below the Crown and ownership. A reform of land tenure in Scotland that addresses the position of the Crown and owners needs also to consider the position of tenants. Just as the nature of the Crown and of ownership are significantly different in Scots law from English law, so the same is the case with leases.

Owners and tenants represent Scotland's landholders, as the only persons defined as capable of the legal occupation of land. While ownership is dependent on holding a title, so leasing land is dependent on holding a valid written document (the lease). The requirement that all leases over 20 years should be recorded, like titles, in the Land Register is also spreading with the Register's coverage. Incidentally, this will eventually make the provisions of the 1449 Leases Act, referred to above, redundant for these leases. It is this ancient Act that converts leases from a personal right (contract) to a real (property) right by securing the lease against landlord succession. For leases over 20 years, this will be guaranteed by registration, while the 1449 Act will still cover shorter leases.

The types of natural and legal persons entitled to hold a lease should be no different from those entitled to hold a title (otherwise, for example, it offers a back door to land occupation). Tenancy and ownership also share other broad characteristics and there will always be a close relationship between the rights of owners and tenants, as the latter derive from the former. The extent, for example, to which tenants have occupation and control of their leased land will determine the extent to which owners are relieved of various liabilities resulting from the use of that land (for example, public safety).

There should also be relatively straightforward differences between the nature of the rights that are deemed to remain with ownership or go with tenancies, as they are fundamentally different arrangements. However, within Scotland's existing system of land tenure, there can be a lack of distinction between owners and tenants. The extent to which crofting tenants have greater rights than some feuars has already been referred to (Chapter 5).

Other examples include the archaic tenure of *tenants at will*. These tenancies are most common in some north-east and Highland villages. Their principal feature is that the tenant (or a predecessor) has built the house and can not be removed so long as they pay rent on the ground involved. They also enjoy customary rights of succession and disposal. The position of *tenants at will* is such that, while labelled tenants, they have already been given the right since 1979 to obtain an owner's title for their holding from their landlord. The holdings of *tenants at will* are also automatically converted into ownerships when they come to be entered into the Land Register.

In addition to such heritable tenancies, other *perpetual leases* also still survive and again contradict the basic character of leases as finite in duration. These and other 'anomalies' (for example, leasehold casualties[3]) tend to be legacies of the long history of feudalism. Within the complexities of that multi-layered system, for example, it has only been over centuries that ownership (or a feu) has emerged from being essentially a tenancy from a superior. Feu duties and other burdens and conditions survive as reminders of this.

While the need to abolish feudal superiorities is widely agreed, there has also long been recognition that this could lead to the emergence in Scotland of an equivalent to the English system of freehold and leasehold. Under such a system, which might be regarded as 'neo-feudal', freeholders can occupy a position similar to superiors. Long leases (for example, 99 or 999 years) not dissimilar to feus are held from them. These are then traded between successive leaseholders for capital values that can be equivalent to those normally associated with property market prices for ownership, even though the buyer is only purchasing the remaining period of the lease.

Some long leases of this kind do exist in Scotland, but are relatively rare.[4] The situation with crofting leases is somewhat similar. These now often change hands for a capital payment unrelated to the value of the tenant's improvements. The payment reflects market demand to obtain the lease, just as others purchase a title. In crofting, of course, it is essentially a perpetual lease (incorporating a right to buy) that is being acquired.

There has long been a broad consensus in Scotland to reject a freehold/leasehold system, because it would negate many of the benefits of abolishing superiorities and bring new disadvantages of its own. As a result of these concerns, some key preventative measures have already been taken (for example, in the Feudal Reform (Scotland) Act, 1974). These include, for example, prohibiting the creation of new residential leases in Scotland of over 20 years duration.

The abolition of feudal tenure in Scotland provides an opportunity to establish more clearly the distinctions between ownership and tenancy, together with the basic framework of the relations between them.

Urban Leases

The law of leases can be seen as consisting of, firstly, an overall legal framework governing all leases and, secondly, a range of specific provisions that are only related to the various different types of leases that exist.

Different types of leases tend to be classified according to the nature of the property and its use. The main traditional division is according to whether leases principally involve buildings (rather misleadingly labelled *urban* leases) or land (*rural* leases). Urban leases are usually subdivided between commercial (shops/offices), industrial (factories) and residential leases, while rural leases also include a number of types such as agricultural and mineral leases (see below).

There are substantial differences in the extent of statutory provisions related to these different types of leases. Amongst urban leases, there is a marked contrast between commercial/industrial leases and residential leases. The former are very largely free of special statutory regulation, while there is a substantial body of legislation covering residential leases. Their position is, however, only intermediate between commercial/industrial and agricultural leases because of the very detailed provisions related to the latter.

A key element of these statutory provisions is whether a particular type of lease has a maximum duration. The legal principle is that all leases should only give temporary rights of occupation and use over the property covered – otherwise the presumption should be that ownership is a more appropriate arrangement. With residential leases, the maximum has been set since 1974 at 20 years.

While limiting the duration of residential leases is a necessary precursor of abolishing superiorities, it also reflects a more long-standing and general presumption against long leases in Scots law (for example, the Long Leases (Scotland) Act 1954). This is based on the principle that leases, as temporary arrangements, should only operate on realistic timescales. In this context, realistic is related to the length of time over which future circumstances might be reasonably anticipated. The provision since 1979 that all leases over 20 years duration require to be recorded in the Land Register is related to the same point.

With residential leases, some leases over 20 years still survive as anomalies. A number of means could be used to remove these. One example would be to follow the type of arrangements used by the 1954 Long Leases Act. This allowed, for a five year period, leases over a certain length (50 years) and older than a set date (1914 – 40 years before) to be converted into feus. Those provisions were over 40 years ago. However, it is their lead that should be followed and not the provisions in the 1985 Law Reform (Miscellaneous Provisions)(Scotland) Act to allow surviving residential leases over 20 years old to continue to be renewed. That 1985 decision could be reversed and all such leases could be converted (like tenants at will and related ground leases) into ownership.

Residential leases over 20 years are already rare and, if they were removed, the only *urban* leases over 20 year that would have to be recorded in the Land Register would be commercial and industrial. Their separate classification is largely a historical legacy, dating from when there tended to be a clearer physical distinction between offices and factories. Recent changes affecting these leases might be considered to be either giving necessary flexibility or moving in the wrong direction – depending on the point of view adopted.

Firstly, *interposed leases*, which had been considered illegal under Scots law, were made legal in 1974. Tenants are generally not allowed to create sub-tenancies. Interposed leases arise, on the other hand, where landlords create an additional tenancy interposed between themselves and the original tenant. The original tenant is thus, with no necessary consent, reduced to a sub-tenant.

A common way in which interposed leases are created is by sale and leaseback. A landlord, for example, sells their property to an investor as a way of raising capital and then leases the property back from the investor. Thus the original landlord remains in occupation of the property as a new tenant to whom the original tenant is a sub-tenant.

Interposed leases have always existed in England and their introduction into Scotland might be seen as a response to commercial pressure. There is an argument, not least on the basis of the consequences of the complexity they spawn, that the financial 'convenience' necessitating interposed leases should remain just a matter of contract law (and not land tenure *per se*).

A second change, in addition to interposed leases, is the ability of tenants to impose new conditions when they assign their lease to a new tenant and for the conditions to be then also enforceable against that tenant's successors. With commercial and industrial leases over 20 years recorded in the Land Register, considerable parallels can be seen between these lease conditions that *run with the land* and feudal burdens and conditions.[5] These lease conditions also count as *land obligations* in terms of the Lands Tribunal's jurisdiction.

This second change results from legislation enacted as recently as 1985. Taken with interposed leases, there is considerable scope for a leasehold system to emerge for commercial and industrial leases. This could replicate many elements of the feudal system and reproduce many of its adverse consequences when that system no longer exists.

Rural Leases

(i) Agricultural

There are two principal types of agricultural leases under Scots law, those held by tenant farmers under Scotland's agricultural holdings legislation and those held by crofters under the crofting legislation. There are also other related types of agricultural tenants defined by statute (for example, the Small Landholder legislation). The

Scottish Land Court, described in Chapter 6, exists solely to deal with matters arising from agricultural leases.

Both the agricultural holdings and crofting legislation date originally from the 1880s. The statutory provisions in each have become notoriously detailed and complex – and there is a sense in which they say more about the social history of the Scottish countryside than modern land use requirements. In both cases, the legislation has been recently consolidated (in the Agricultural Holdings (Scotland) Act 1991 and the Crofting (Scotland) Act 1993). This has opened up the scope for rationalisation and is also a useful precursor for reforms.

Crofting tenants have more flexibility than tenant farmers in the uses they can make of the land and buildings on their holdings. A basic problem, however, is that both leases are 'agricultural leases' and the tenants' options are essentially limited by the definition of *agriculture* in the Acts. This isolation of agriculture can be traced back to the nature of medieval land grants. It is at odds with both contemporary standards of integrated land use (for example, the management of trees and woodlands) and the requirements of rural development more generally (such as diversification into non-agricultural activities).

Crofters' rights are not only greater than those of agricultural tenants, but in many respects equivalent to those of tenants at will (see above) and some feuars. One aspect of the distinctive position of crofters is that they only pay rent on the un-improved value of their land. They also already have a partial right to buy and, at one level, there is a strong logic in giving crofters the status and rights of owners. The particular option for crofters should, however, reflect community traditions and the legacies of indigenous Gaelic tenure. Thus, crofters might remain tenants under reformed crofting legislation, while at the same time constituting part of their own landlord as part of some form of community trust. The right to buy of individual crofters might also be extended to crofting townships and from in-bye land to common grazings.[6] The current right to buy was brought in by crofting legislation in 1976 and has not been without its problems. Amongst other reforms related to the 1976 legislation could be measures that enable new crofts to be created straightforwardly.

There is also a widely recognised need to reform the agricultural holdings legislation. Two key issues are the form of a new arrangement for leasing farm land and the fate of existing agricultural tenancies. There appears a broad measure of agreement amongst key parties that, *firstly*, the new arrangement should represent a reduction in specific statutory provisions and a significant move into the flexibility of contract law, and that, *secondly*, existing tenant farmers should not be disadvantaged by any changes.

While it is considered socially desirable to protect the interests of these tenants, preserving their status quo will not halt the rapid decline in their numbers over recent decades and do nothing to promote integrated land use. There would appear a public interest case at least to broaden the definition of agriculture that they are operating under. This could allow them greater scope to meet modern circumstances by diversifying their business activities to broaden their income base and so increase their security. More radical proposals could involve enabling these tenants, or the more long-standing families amongst them, to convert into owner-occupiers.[7] These tenants already have statutory rights of succession, many have been tenant farmers for generations and such a proposal could be seen as following the precedent and pattern of the 1954 Long Leases (Scotland) Act (see above).

A new type of agricultural lease could take a number of different forms. Two important aspects here, however, are the duration and scope of the lease.

A maximum of 20 years duration would avoid the requirement to enter them in the Land Register, with associated implications. Twenty years also fits well for a land use lease, as the period of 'reasonable anticipation', and coincides with the duration that has already emerged as the most common in existing farm partnerships. It would also have historical associations with the traditional 19 year term of Scottish agriculture.

With regard to the scope of any new type of agricultural lease in Scotland, the permitted activities should not be so constrained as at present. Current agricultural leases are so narrowly defined, they might be seen as an anomaly that goes against the 'exclusive occupation' normally required to constitute a lease in Scots law. The tenants under any new arrangement should be able to meet modern standards of integrated land use. Activities such as woodland management and public access/recreation management should automatically come within their sphere, albeit with appropriate safeguards for landlords' interests. The same might apply to other diversification opportunities, including the uses that can be made of farm, or former farm, buildings.

At one level, much of this could be achieved by simply reforming the definition of agriculture in the relevant statutes. A reduction in statutory provisions would also give greater flexibility to allow for tenant activities that are adapted to local circumstances.

(ii) Forestry

Forestry rights go with the general rights of ownership over land and can not be held as a separate tenement or right of ownership. The one apparent exception to this is when someone buys 'standing timber' from a land owner. This is sometimes construed to give ownership of the standing trees, but it should be clearly established that the purchase of the timber is simply a contractual agreement to fell and remove the trees.[8]

There have been 'forestry leases' since the 1960s. These have been for bare land afforestation, usually over a relatively long term (for example, 60–80 years or more) and based on the idea that the lease will end at the stage of bare land again when the crop is clear felled. This latter presumption is already unrealistic in terms of the forestry standards enforced through statutory felling licences.

There is no more validity to the concept of single land use forestry leases than there is to narrow agricultural leases. In future, agricultural and forestry leases might in many ways be seen as permutations on the same basic form of land lease, with their difference being variations of character and emphasis in the contractual details agreed between the parties. All such leases would conventionally start and end with valuations, avoiding any bare land considerations for forestry.

(iii) Hunting and Fishing

The modernisation of land tenure provides an opportunity to clarify the often confusing and archaic terminology associated with the rights of land owners in Scotland to take (kill or capture) certain species of wild animals on their land.

There is, for example, frequent reference to the right to take 'game', but it is variously defined in different Acts and there is no contemporary agreement as to which species are covered by this label.[9] The rights of owners also cover species that have never been considered 'game' and really, in line with the influence of modern legislation, the whole subject should be viewed as a part of wildlife management. While the owners' rights are also commonly referred to as 'sporting rights', this traditional label is too narrow in its focus and misleading in its emphasis. The conventional term internationally for these wildlife management rights is 'hunting rights' and this is used here. For some, this label is still too closely associated with the predominantly English activity of hunting foxes with horses and hounds.

The real issue is the legal character of hunting rights. The ownership of land does not convey 'ownership' over wild animals, but only a right to prevent others from taking them (see Chapter 9). This right is not exclusive (for example, agricultural tenants have a statutory right to protect crops from deer and some other species) and also only covers the species that can be taken lawfully subject to the prescribed legal conditions (for example, only during defined seasons and by certain methods). Hunting rights are thus only a restricted 'incident' of the ownership of land.

There is a legacy of ambiguity about the nature of this 'incident' that needs to be rationalised as part of the modernisation of land tenure. This principally involves clarifying that the ownership of hunting rights can not be separated at all from the ownership of land, whether as a full separate tenement or as some form of reservation, burden or servitude.[10]

The ambiguity has principally resulted from the long-standing pressure by land owning interests to promote hunting rights as being capable of separation from the land and so more financially valuable. One result of this was the overthrowing by Lord Inglis in a Court of Session case in 1881 of the previously well-established legal principle that the incidental nature of hunting rights precluded them from being the subject of a lease. Clarification that the ownership of hunting rights 'runs with the land' could be linked to rationalisation of the scope to lease them. A first element in this could be to prohibit long leases and restrict any hunting lease to a maximum of 20 years, as the period of 'realistic expectation' (see above). Long leases (for example, 99 years) have been a rich source of legal disputes and pose particular problems for changing patterns and standards of land use. A second element would be to review the extent to which hunting rights can form a separate lease.

A lease has to be of land, otherwise it is simply a personal contract or licence to hunt. Similarly, a lease should also carry occupation of the land, rather than just authority to carry out a particular activity over the land.[11] This could be taken, for example, as challenging the scope to have a hunting lease over land already covered by an agricultural or crofting tenancy. More generally, many instances that are currently said in conventional terms to be 'sporting leases', could just be considered in legal terms to be a licence to hunt.

In a reformed system of land tenure, hunting rights could either be retained 'in hand' by the owner directly, exercised under licence or else form part of a lease that was not exclusively for hunting, but which incorporated other uses by virtue of being a lease of land (for example, see ii above).

Most of the above could apply equally to fishing, which is essentially still 'hunting' but for different wild species in a different medium. There are though two key distinctions. Firstly, salmon fishing is accepted as a legally separate tenement and the Freshwater and Salmon Fisheries (Scotland) Act 1976 also made leases of trout fishings effective against landlord successors. However, both the status of salmon fishing (see Chapter 13) and the statutory framework provided by the 1976 Act could usefully be reviewed to promote more sustainable natural resource management.[12]

(iv) Mining and Quarrying

The framework within which mineral leases occur could be changed significantly by proposals to modernise and reform the ownership of mineral rights. The proposals would increase the proportion of mineral exploitation under lease or licence, as opposed to ownership (see Chapter 9).

These proposals would remove the geological strata below the surface layer from the sphere of ownership, preclude the appropriation of the seabed and its surface minerals into ownership and also end the ability to own minerals as a separate tenement. Thus all mining in the marine environment and elsewhere below the surface layer, would be through a lease or licence.

The proposal to end the creation of mineral rights as a separate tenement would also, of itself, resolve many of the confusions and ambiguities that have existed as to which minerals were being conveyed (see Chapter 9). It would also draw a more logical and beneficial distinction between rights of ownership and rights of use. The exploitation of the surface layer minerals would thus be either through a lease or under licence.

The scope for interposed leases and sub-leasing generally could be avoided, with any ambition to involve additional parties in the operations met through contracts. In addition, the leases could be limited to the 20 year period of 'realistic expectation'. This would also enhance the benefits of retaining a link between mineral rights and the ownership of land by providing an opportunity for the nature of the lease to be reviewed periodically.

Contracts

In Scotland's system of land tenure, the requirements to constitute a lease are legally defined (as explained at the start of this chapter). Below that, is a right of *licence*: "a contractual right to the use or occupation of the heritable property of another not constituting a tenancy in the legal sense".[13]

There are thus, below the Crown, three basic levels of use and occupation: ownership, tenancy and licence. Each has its own types of document: titles, leases and contracts. If the legal requirements to constitute a particular level are not fulfilled, the rights of use and occupation fall to the next level: ownership to lease; lease to licence.

The broad principles distinguishing these levels are well established. There is, however, the opportunity in modernising land tenure to clarify the actual frontiers between them. This has already been illustrated between ownership and tenancy with examples like kindly tenants and tenants at will. Issues also arise between lease and licence.

A common instance that can cause some confusion is *timesharing* (for example, of holiday homes or salmon fishings). The person who acquires a timeshare has the right to occupy the property exclusively for a particular period. The right is generally 'in perpetuity' and can be sold as a capital asset for gain or disposed of in other conventional ways. This creates the impression of some form of common ownership, but in fact the arrangement does not even constitute a lease.[14]

In this situation, the owner of a timeshare does not have a *real right* but simply a personal right under a contract with the actual owner of the property (usually the timeshare company). Ways have been suggested by which it might be possible to constitute timeshares as leases and potentially, perpetual leases.[15] The scope for this in theory does not, however, suggest it would be good in practice because of the arguments outlined above against long leases, particularly for natural resource use activities like fishing. The growth of sub-leasing in the commercial sector is another frontier where the grey area between leases and contracts is an issue, as explained earlier in this chapter.

The law of leases involves contract law because leases are a form of contract. A right of licence, by contrast, is entirely within contract law. It can be considered outwith land tenure as such and thus subject to 'freedom of contract'. Licence holders are not statutory landholders and thus do not relieve these landholders of particular liabilities and obligations that befall their status. Correspondingly, the lack of 'occupation' by licence holders is reflected in the fact that there can be many overlapping licences, but not leases, over the same area of land. Crucially, the terms of a licence holder's contract do not 'run with the land' – they are a personal contract and, unlike leases, they are not effective against the landholder's successors.

There are many examples of types of licence arrangements in each natural resource use sector, for example, crop sharing, contract farming or in the activities of forestry investment/management companies. In some sectors, the use of licence arrangements could be promoted to some extent over the use of leases (for example, with sporting and mineral rights – see earlier in this chapter). There may be a need, however, for a clearer framework of rules than exists at present in particular instances (for example, agriculture). These rules could come within the sphere of the Lands Tribunal for Scotland (see Chapter 6).

Licence arrangements can involve payments in either direction between the licence holder and landholder – a licence holder being paid to do some task or paying to be able to do some activities. The arrangements can also involve payments to the landholder not to do certain things. This latter category is most commonly associated with environmental payments at present, for example, to manage special habitats in particular ways. It highlights wider concerns, however, about the need to maintain a clear boundary over the types of contractual commitments that can be imposed on successors.

The Forestry Commission's Woodland Grant Scheme is a straightforward example of contracts with landholders, where the contracts have to be formally taken on by the landholders' successors. If they are not, there can be a liability to repay all or some of the FC's grants. Other more confidential government arrangements might be presumed to be on a similar basis (for example, tax exemptions under the Inheritance Tax Act 1984 for land owners in exchange for public access or some other public benefits over land).

In other instances, payments to land owners are identified as conditional on the attachment of particular conditions to the owner's title to the land involved, for example, over public access.[16] This is to secure the conditions from the payer's point of view, so that the conditions run with the land and are effective against the land owner's successors. The conditions thus become a burden on the land. The conditions may be imposed for a finite period or left open-ended (i.e. as a perpetual burden).

In these situations, while the payments may ostensibly be 'grants', they are essentially being used to buy future management options on the land involved. They thus prejudice those future options for good or bad. The opportunity to create these types of title conditions should be severely constrained, as with 'post-feudal' perpetual title burdens generally (for example, see Chapter 13). The scope of contracts over land should be clarified and, as part of this, brought more within the 20 year frame of realistic expectations as this applies to leases and other topics.

Contracts over land should be the arena of flexible, short term arrangements and not become the source of what could turn out to be long term problems.

Conclusions from Section 4

Chapter 11 Rights to Own and Dispose of Land

• There is scope to refine the types of natural and legal persons that can own land in Scotland and to bring the law of succession to land into line with that for all other types of property.
• Private property rights to intervene in the land market (such as pre-emption) could be phased out and the public interest safeguarded better by regulation similar to that in the companies market.

Chapter 12 Arrangements for Shared and Common Ownership

• The framework of arrangements for different forms of co-ownership could be clarified and the different types of genuinely common land that can exist could be clearly established.

Chapter 13 The Relationships Between Different Owners

• The authority of owners to impose burdens on other owners through their title deeds could be ended and all perpetual charges, such as feu duties, could also be abolished.
• The existing system of burdens and conditions could be replaced with an equitable system, independent of the terms of title deeds and dependent on laws of neighbourhood, such as common interest and nuisance.

Chapter 14 The Leasing of Land

• Land is the only form of property which can be leased in Scots law and there is a substantial body of law on the leasing of land, which deals with many of the same types of topics as the laws related to ownership.
• The boundaries between ownership and leasing, as well as leasing and contracts that do not constitute leases, could be clarified and each of the different types of leases that can exist could in its own ways be reformed.

SECTION FIVE

Land Tenure Reform

CHAPTER FIFTEEN

A Reform Programme

The previous sections of this book have provided a wide ranging and exploratory review of Scotland's system of land tenure. The first section set current moves to reform the existing system in context, while the second outlined the basic nature and scope of the system. The next two sections then described in turn the main rights currently held in Scotland's land by the Crown, representing the public interest, and by all owners, whether private persons or public bodies. This fifth section looks to the future.

The purpose of the first four sections was to provide a 'map' of the current system as a contribution to discussions about reforming the system. As a prompt to further discussion, many suggestions were also made to highlight elements of the current system that could be changed to create a system more supportive of contemporary values for economic development, social well-being and environmental stewardship. This chapter pulls together some of the main suggested changes.

The proposed reforms are presented in summary form below. They are not listed in order of priority or their relative importance. They follow a broadly similar sequence to the description given in the previous sections and cover the rights and interests held within the system by the Crown, owners and tenants. Their overall coherence and significance as part of a package of reforms is discussed in the next chapter.

The proposals are labelled here as a reform 'programme' to emphasise that a series of measures will be required to modernise and reform Scotland's system of land tenure. They are not a refined selection of issues listed as a blueprint for reform or some sort of yes/no checklist. A number of the proposals are already being examined by government as potential reforms. These are at different stages of development, from initial consultations to draft legislation.

Adding further topics to this work and taking each through the sequences of stages from initial consideration to enactment, illustrates how an ongoing reform programme could be built up in the Scottish Parliament.

- *The Crown's Feudal Position*

Proposals to abolish the Crown's feudal position as *Paramount Superior* as part of abolishing all superiorities (see below). This could include extinguishing the Crown's other identities based on feudal titles to land (for example, as Baron of Renfrew and Prince of Scotland), while not excluding the possibility that these identities could be re-constituted as honorary or ceremonial titles unrelated to property rights.

- *Rights Held in Trust*

Proposals to re-name and define in contemporary terms the *Regalia* or Crown Rights as rights held in trust for the public (people of Scotland) in the name of the Crown, and with all authority over the management and use of these rights vested in Parliament. This could include, amongst subsidiary aspects, removing a Royal prerogative against the statutory regulation and designation of land.

- *Public Trust Lands*

Proposals to clarify the areas of Scotland held in trust for the public by consolidating the position in the marine environment and redefining the position above and below ground, while limiting the retained areas on land to parts of the foreshore and specified 'ancient sites' of national importance. This could include preventing the alienation of parts of the seabed, further areas of foreshore and any salmon fishing and mineral rights still held in trust.

- *Crown Estate*

Proposals to rename the Crown Estate to reflect its public identity and to transfer all its regulation and administration to democratically accountable bodies. This would involve a phased replacement of the Crown Estate Commission in Scotland, including divestment of its commercial properties and rural estates and the redefinition of the responsibilities to be passed to successor bodies.

- *Separate Ownerships*

Proposals to prevent the creation of new separate tenements or ownerships in mineral rights or salmon fishings, whether by the Crown or existing owners. This could include the redefinition of the nature and constitution of mineral rights.

- *Wildlife Resources*

Proposals to consolidate the legal basis of the public interest in wildlife by converting its status in law from *res nullius* (owned by nobody) to *res communis* (communal asset). This could include abolishing the concepts of royal animals and game species, the re-definition of sporting rights and the reform of freshwater fishing rights.

- *Public Access*

Proposals to improve the statutory framework of different types of public access rights. This could include updating and redefining access to the foreshore, rights of navigation in freshwater rivers and lochs, streamlining the provisions for Public Rights of Way, and establishing a conditional right of 'freedom to roam' over land.

- *Feudal Superiorities*

Proposals to abolish all feudal superiorities and associated rights and interests. This could include, amongst subsidiary aspects, extinguishing all feudal identities based on titles to land (for example, Barons and Hereditary Keepers), while not excluding the possibility that some could be re-constituted as honorary or ceremonial titles unrelated to property rights.

- *Form of Tenure*

Proposals to convert all feus and other existing types of titles to land (for example, under alloidal, udal and other forms of tenures) to a new single basic form of direct ownership or tenure. This could include converting categories such as tenants at will and kindly tenants, as well as other perpetual leaseholds, into conventional ownership.

- *Register of Titles*

Proposals to establish a comprehensive map-based and publicly accessible register of all titles to land. This could include refining the definition of who can hold a title to land and requiring a registered legally responsible person resident in Scotland for all title holders resident elsewhere.

- *Charges and Conditions*

Proposals to abolish all feu duties and all related perpetual private charges on land (for example, multures, stipends and teinds). This could also include abolishing leasehold casualties and ending the private regulation of some owners by other owners through the imposition of real burdens in their titles to land.

- *Neighbourhood Laws*

Proposals to establish a coherent framework of land conditions that are independent of titles to land and enable all land owners to safeguard their legitimate interests against the actions of other owners. This could include revising the laws of tenement, nuisance, common interest and servitudes.

- *Inheritance Rights*

Proposals to reform the laws of succession to give spouses and children the same legal rights with respect to inheritances in land as they already enjoy for all other forms of property. This could include also abolishing the last vestiges of the laws of entail in Scotland.

- *Market Intervention*

Proposals to prohibit the creation of new private rights of redemption and pre-emption affecting the sales of land and to phase out these existing rights. This could include introducing a government right of pre-emption and also options to intervene in the land market either to ensure new owners meet certain management standards or else to allow for alternative bids.

• *Leases*

Proposals to limit sub-letting in urban leases, to phase out the remaining residential leases over 20 years, to prohibit sporting leases over that duration and to reform agricultural and crofting leases. This latter could include, for example, rationalising the crofting legislation, enabling the creation of new crofts and extending a conditional right to buy to common grazings.

The 15 headings above each contain more than one specific proposal and the overall number of proposals, combined with the summary form of their presentation, can obscure the way in which such proposals might contribute to a coherent programme of land tenure reform. This process and the overall potential of such a programme are considered in the next chapter but, at this stage, a number of general features of the list can be noted.

Firstly, the proposals span the three levels of tenure within the system, as represented by the public rights vested in the Crown and the respective rights that go with the ownership and the leasing of land. The proposals demonstrate some of the opportunities to modernise and reform both the nature of the rights at each level and the relationships between the levels – between the public interest and the interests of owners and between the interests of owners and of tenants.

Secondly, there are two central aspects to the proposals, both of which are explored more fully in the next chapter. The first is reforming the position of the Crown and the rights held in its name in trust for the public or people of Scotland. Central to this is the distinction between the Crown as a constitutional or symbolic representative of the public and the responsibility of Parliament for these rights as the democratic expression of the actual public interest at any point in time. One part of this is reforming the administration of the current Crown Estate. However, the precise nature of the rights retained in all land also needs to be established definitively as part of determining more clearly the ways in which the ownership of land in Scotland is conditional on the public interest.

The second central aspect involves reforming the nature of land ownership within that conditional, public interest context. A basic part of this reform is establishing a new and equitable, fully recorded system of titles to land in which the capacity of some owners to impose burdens or conditions on other owners through their title deeds is replaced by all owners having equal rights to defend their interests against other owners through laws of good neighbourhood.

CHAPTER SIXTEEN

Creating A New System

Developing a Reform Programme

The abolition of feudal tenure is a fairly obvious and nicely symbolic starting point for land tenure reform and the government is already committed to bringing forward draft legislation to achieve this in the Scottish Parliament. Work is also in hand within government on a number of other topics covered in the list of proposals given in the previous chapter. The Scottish Law Commission, for example, is due to submit proposals on reforming leasehold casualties and the law of tenement, while Scottish Natural Heritage is to report on the requirements for legislation to improve public access and the Scottish Office is working on proposals to transfer the regulatory role of the Crown Estate Commission in coastal waters to local authorities.

These topics and others are already starting to build up the basis of a land tenure reform programme in the Scottish Parliament. Further topics will be added in the lead up to the Parliament. An immediate candidate is, for example, land registration. The existing progress towards bringing all parts of Scotland within the scope of the Land Register could be accelerated on a self-financing basis without legislation. However, enabling legislation will be needed for the compulsory production of titles that will be required to complete the registration of all titles to land in Scotland. While a comprehensive and publicly accessible Register will have many practical and economic benefits, the enabling legislation to achieve that will have its own symbolic value as the key step to answering once and for all the potent question of who owns Scotland.

It will take some years to have the completed Land Register up and running, even if the enabling legislation and arrangements to manage the final compulsory production of titles have been prepared by the time the Parliament is in position. However, many of the other potential aspects of land tenure reform will also need to be spread over some years, from the initial consideration and consultation on a topic to draft legislation, enactment and implementation with, in some cases, the phasing out of old arrangements while new ones are phased in. Thus it might be expected that at any point in time, there will be a number of different land reform measures being advanced through various stages and that they will add over time to a rolling programme of reforms. This pattern is already emerging even with the limited number of issues already identified by the government. When the Scottish Parliament is established, some topics will be at a draft legislation stage and others only at initial consultation. The Parliament will then be able to add its own choice of topics.

This type of approach is incremental rather than revolutionary, even if the culminative results could profoundly change land tenure in Scotland. The approach is essentially a practical way of tackling a large and complex subject area. The approach allows, amongst other advantages, different reform measures to be taken forward in the right sequence and to be co-ordinated and integrated with other measures. This is necessary as part of reforming an overall system of land tenure in which all the different elements need to be compatible and consistent with each other within a coherent whole.

This process of modernisation and reform will in some senses be unending. There will always be a need to update the system of land tenure to meet changing circumstances and requirements over time. The problem at present is the exceptionally limited extent to which this updating process has gone on in the past, not least due to the isolation of Scots law from a legislature directly concerned with it. The Scottish Parliament will provide the opportunity for a concentrated phase of land tenure reform to catch up on the many different aspects that need to be tackled.

While the debate about the potential ingredients of that pulse of reform is well underway, it is still at a relatively early stage. The prospect of reform in the new Parliament is acting as an incentive to giving greater attention to land tenure and a stimulus to new thinking. As the debate progresses and becomes more informed, so the nature of the various problems to be dealt with and the solutions required will become more clearly established than at present.

Types of Changes

The system of land tenure is, as highlighted in this book, simply a mechanism. Determining the problems with it comes, in the first instance, not just from looking at the system itself, but from examining what are judged its adverse economic, social and environmental consequences. This book has not focused on identifying those problems. Instead, as reflected in the structure of the book, the approach has been to set out a description of the system to help provide a framework for discussions about it.

The book does contain a series of proposals for ways in which the current system of land tenure could be changed to give a system better able to accommodate and support the economic, social and environmental aims of society. However, these proposals are suggested as a prompt to further discussion and not presented as an agenda for change. The proposals illustrate the scope for reform and can be grouped under two main themes: rationalisation and re-focusing.

(i) Rationalisation

Scotland's system of land tenure, like such systems generally, has to be extensive and flexible enough to deal with very diverse issues and circumstances. However, for essentially historical reasons, Scotland's existing system is unnecessarily voluminous and complex. The proposals suggested to rationalise this can be equated, somewhat over simplistically, with a *tidy out* and a *tidy up*.

Firstly, as identified throughout the book, there are many largely archaic elements of the existing system that could be more or less swept away. The list extends from superiorities and feu duties, other feudal titles, charges and tenures, to the laws of entail, private rights of redemption and pre-emption, and a range of fairly obscure topics like 'royal animals'. Secondly, a wide range of other topics are identified within the system where the legal position is uncertain and could be usefully resolved. These uncertainties often result from the system's long history and the extent to which its development has been based on legal precedent in recent centuries.

All of this rationalisation is also linked to the scope more generally to clarify the structure and contents of Scotland's system of land tenure, right down to the concepts and language being used. These changes could potentially be carried out reasonably uncontroversially with little prejudice to existing legal interests in land. This lack of direct or material impact should not, however, lead to the worth of these reforms being undervalued. They would make the system more straightforward, understandable and efficient and, as discussed, bring wider benefits to the owners of land and society generally.

(ii) Re-focusing

The second strand of proposals are those that go beyond simple rationalisation. They are intended more directly to produce a system better suited to current circumstances and contemporary requirements. This re-focusing is seen in terms of making the system more supportive of economic development, social well-being and environmental stewardship. These wider proposals demonstrate that there is considerable opportunity to modernise and reform the system of land tenure in Scotland in ways that would benefit both public and private interests.

The rights and interests attached to ownership would, for example, be freed from the complex burdens and conditions that some owners can impose on other owners. All land owners would hold their land on an equitable basis, with stronger rights to safeguard their legitimate interests against the actions of others. The rights and interests of all owners would also be more clearly protected against inappropriate erosion by the state. The proposals would also lead to increases in the numbers of owners. Ownership is central to the system of land tenure and these improvements in the position of ownership would, as discussed, be in the public interest.

At the same time, the position of the public interest *within* the system of land tenure would be promoted by modernising and reforming the rights and interests to be retained by the Crown. There are two main aspects to this. The first involves continuing the long-standing trend of reducing the *direct* responsibilities of the Crown within the land tenure system by transferring them to democratically accountable public bodies. The second aspect, in contrast, highlights the importance of recognising and retaining in contemporary terms, the rights and interests that are held in trust by the Crown for the people of Scotland. These rights form the basis of land tenure in Scotland. They set the context for the rights that go with ownership and represent the public interest in the balance of public and private interests within land tenure.

Position of the Crown

Previous chapters have distinguished clearly between two different approaches required to reform the position of the Crown in Scotland's land tenure system. On one hand, the abolition of the Crown's feudal and proprietorial rights. On the other hand, safeguarding and giving modern expression to the Crown's sovereign rights.

At first, the idea of a continuing importance for the Crown in land tenure may appear very strange to many people. The assumption amongst most members of the two main types of professional interests involved with land tenure reform, lawyers and rural developers, appears to have been that there should be more or less no role left for the Crown. However, lawyers, who are mainly urban based, tend to approach land tenure from a fairly narrow, conveyancing perspective, while rural developers, who are mainly Highland based, tend to approach land tenure from a wider land reform perspective. For the lawyers, the situation has appeared reasonably straightforward. The Crown's position as Paramount Superior is abolished and there is then no need for the Crown to be directly involved in titles to land at all.[1] For the group with a wider interest in land reform, the Crown's continuing position as Paramount Superior is seen as a symbol of the feudal system and the existing pattern of land ownership, and is associated for many with the Monarch, Balmoral Estates and the Crown Estate Commission.[2]

From these two perspectives, the emphasis on the Crown in this book could initially appear misplaced. However, it should first be recognised that the role of the Crown outlined here is not at odds with the arguments of either group. The proposals suggested (for example, abolishing the paramount superiority and reforming the Crown Estate Commission) would address both their agendas. The question is the surviving identity and position of the Crown once its feudal identity and rights have been removed. The issue, as it has been variously expressed by others, is to take care not to throw out the public interest baby with the very dirty feudal bathwater.[3]

This book highlights the importance of the sovereign rights still vested in the Crown in Scotland and how the distinct nature of these rights in Scotland provides a public interest foundation to the system of land tenure. Statements of this position are not new.[4] However, it has only started to be more widely recognised in recent years, particularly following references to it in the prominent series of McEwen Lectures on Land Tenure in Scotland.[5] A part of this appreciation is that these sovereign rights do not leave undemocratic powers with the Crown. They are a set of constitutional and legal principles which define the public interest in Scotland's land and to which Parliament gives contemporary expression at any point in time. Parliament is thus responsible for determining and actually representing the public interest. The Crown's position is a constitutional one and is only representative in the sense of 'standing for' or 'symbolising' the enduring values of the public interest. It happens to be the Crown that is involved simply because Britain is a constitutional monarchy. If Scotland became a republic with an elected president, then these rights would adhere, as in the USA for example, to the presidency.

The positive values of this analysis tend to find a sympathetic response from those interested in wider land reforms in Scotland, because the position it gives to the public interest coincides with their own pursuit of the public interest. Many land reformers, when they have complained about the feudal pattern of land ownership in Scotland, have been surprised to discover that the system of land ownership is actually feudal in a legal and technical sense. It is perhaps a more pleasant surprise to realise that there is a legal and technical basis within the system for the populist view that, in the final analysis, 'the land belongs to the people of Scotland'.

This view has not been so readily adopted by many lawyers involved with land tenure reform. Their focus has been on conveyancing and has been preoccupied with private relationships (for example, between superiors and vassals; benefited and servient properties; and landlords and tenants), not the relationships between public and private interests. Indeed, the proposals from the

Scottish Law Commission that feudalism should be replaced with a system of *absolute* ownership seem to convey all the wrong messages and imply that the public interest could be worse off than at present. The term *absolute* is not one that will appear in any legislation and the Scottish Law Commission have been careful to say that abolishing the Crown's paramount superiority will not in any way affect the Crown's other identities, roles, rights and interests.[6] However, the nature of these within the land tenure system, to the extent that they are referred to, tends to come across as a somewhat disparate list of miscellaneous particular rights (such as those involving the public right of navigation at sea, treasure trove, or the foreshore). The public interest can appear to be represented only by administrative law interacting with the private rights of land tenure or ownership. Attention has yet to be turned to the Crown as representing a coherent and underlying framework of rights for the public interest within the land tenure system itself.

Constitutional Issues

A fresh perspective on the position of the public interest in land tenure through the Crown has not been helped by the divides that tend to exist, both in universities and elsewhere in the legal establishment, between public and private law. Then, beyond that, within the public law sector, questions of sovereignty and the Crown are matters which need to be progressed by developments in constitutional law. The emergence over recent decades of a distinct and growing body of work on Scottish constitutional law has already been commented on (see page 43). However, the extent of that progress appears to have been overtaken by the political moves to establish a democratically elected legislating parliament in Scotland.

The new Parliament is widely recognised as the most significant constitutional development for Scotland since the former Parliament became amalgamated with the English Parliament at Westminster over 290 years ago. It is recognised that, constitutionally, the new Parliament will not be the same as the old one, which operated within Scotland as an independent state. However, the prospect of the new Parliament has opened up questions about its actual constitutional status and this, in turn, has raised wider questions about the nature of the Union between Scotland and England in 1707. Some of these questions were set out in the 1997 British Academy Lecture under a title that alludes to the nature of these issues: "The English Constitution, the British State and the Scottish Anomaly".[7]

The focus of this debate is Scotland's national sovereignty. The question is not whether Scotland is a sovereign nation or whether that sovereignty is based on the sovereignty of the people. These facts are reasonably established. The issue is the relationship between that sovereignty and the doctrine of the sovereignty of parliament that derives from the English constitution and prevails at Westminster. The tension between these different sovereignties was highlighted during the 1997 Devolution Referendum by the seriousness of the debate in which Scotland secured agreement that, firstly, the Westminster Parliament could not constitutionally close down the Scottish Parliament against the wishes of the majority of the Scottish people and that secondly, if a majority of the Scottish people sought independence or a change to Union settlement with England, then Westminster would be constitutionally obliged to come to terms with the will of the Scottish people.

These issues of principle illustrate that, while there is no doubt that the new Parliament will be a devolved parliament under the authority of the UK Parliament, the establishment and existence of the Scottish Parliament is likely to provide a major impetus to constitutional law in Scotland. This can be expected to lead to fuller interpretations and more contemporary statements on the nature and implications of Scotland's sovereignty. Any such exercise will involve focusing on Scots law itself as, both in its survival as a distinct legal system and in the content of some of its provisions, Scots law has been crucial as a refuge of national sovereignty. The system of land tenure has special importance within this because of its relationship, as described earlier, to control over territory. Correspondingly, the development of the constitutional arguments will strengthen and underpin recognition of the role of sovereignty and the Crown in representing the public interest within the system of land tenure.

Devolved Matters

The legislation establishing the Scottish Parliament will reserve constitutional matters to Westminster, while providing the new

Parliament with extensive authority to legislate on aspects of Scots law. This raises the issue whether there is any potential difficulty between these two provisions within the context of land tenure. One aspect of this is that it is often not clear what is and is not considered a constitutional matter, particularly given the uncertainty engendered by the lack of a written British constitution. In this situation, there can be a danger that anything involving the 'Crown' might be construed as constitutional and therefore reserved.

The proposition that the Scottish Parliament will remove what is usually referred to as the Crown's 'ultimate ownership' of Scotland, might appear to many people as an inherently constitutional matter. However, the government and others have no difficulty with the idea that the Scottish Parliament will abolish the Crown's Paramount Superiority as a part of reforming Scots land law. It might therefore be presumed that other components of the Crown's rights in land under Scots law, known as the regalia, can also be reformed by the Parliament together with those related aspects of the Royal prerogative that are defined in Scots law, such as how the Crown may acquire property or make contracts in Scotland.[8]

The scope for confusion on such matters is, however, illustrated by the position with the Crown Estate Commission (CEC). On one hand, the Crown rights that form the Crown Estate in Scotland are all defined by Scots law (for example, the nature of the foreshore and rights over it). Therefore, the position with reforms might appear the same as that for the paramount superiority. However, on the other hand, the CEC was constituted under UK legislation. This, combined with the significance of the Crown Estate in England and its ties there with the Duchy of Cornwall, mean that legislation relating to the Crown Estate or Crown Estate Commissioners tends to be seen as a constitutional matter at Westminster. This is reinforced by the long-standing presumption amongst constitutional lawyers in England that Scotland was essentially incorporated into the English constitution at the Union in 1707.[9] As part of this, there is little awareness amongst them that, despite there being one Monarch, the Crown can have different identities and rights in England and Scotland.

At present, the draft legislation to establish the Scottish Parliament, the Scotland Bill, specifically cites the CEC as a reserved matter. Therefore, while the fate of the Secretary of State for Scotland's existing power of direction over the CEC is still uncertain, it appears that the CEC will not be one of the UK or GB bodies for which the Scottish Parliament can choose to establish a separate Scottish successor.[10] A more pressing issue is the extent to which the Parliament will have the jurisdiction to legislate on the CEC's duties and functions within Scotland. The government itself has said it is to bring forward proposals for legislation in the Scottish Parliament to transfer the CEC's regulatory responsibilities over fish farms in coastal waters to local authorities.[11] This widely supported move is indicative of how public policy might be frustrated if the Scottish Parliament does not have adequate authority to legislate over the CEC. No doubt the position will be made clear as the legislation to establish the Parliament progresses. However, it is an issue that would not have arisen if the CEC in Scotland had been correctly, as has been explained earlier, constituted separately under Scots law in 1961.

Culminative Impact of Reforms

Major reforms to the CEC's responsibilities and functions in Scotland would be a telling change for the Scottish Parliament to make. Such reforms, which would potentially be very widely supported, would be a clear signal of the Parliament's commitment to tackle the land issue and would offer the scope to demonstrate the values behind that commitment. The reforms could reassert the public's rights in the areas and rights currently managed by the CEC, place their management under more direct democratic control and redefine the aims of management away from narrow financial returns to a responsibility for the sustainable development of the Crown Estate.

Many of the other possible reforms outlined in Chapter 15 would also have their own individual special significance. The impact of many of these measures by themselves might not seem very great. However, these types of reforms need to be seen in context, including an awareness of the issues that land tenure will not address directly. Many of the most immediate and marked improvements in rural development and natural resource use can be achieved by measures that do not involve or depend on land tenure reform.

Public sector grant schemes, for example, can be adjusted (for example, greater cross compliance between schemes) to promote many different benefits, or administrative initiatives taken, like the recent establishment of a Community Land Unit at Highlands and Islands Enterprise. This Unit is to increase the extent of community land ownership in the Highlands, based on the benefits this is expected to bring. However, in this, the communities replace the former owners as the owners; this does not change the system of ownership nor does it depend on changes to that system. Also, while land tenure reforms could have an effect on the pattern or distribution of land ownership over time, it is other measures that could have a more direct impact on reducing the current concentration of private land ownership (for example, targeted taxation and regulation of the land market).

The overall significance of the types of land tenure reforms outlined is their underlying and culminative influence. Together they would create a 'new system' of land tenure that both directly reflects the values of social democracy, economic development and environmental stewardship and, vitally, provides a template that is more supportive than the current system of other measures to achieve these goals. It is in that context that many of the apparently minor land tenure reforms identified during the course of this book (for example, sweeping away many archaic elements of the current system), become particularly worth doing.

It is also in this context that the position of the Crown is most significant and why such importance has been attached to it in this book. This position establishes that the system of land tenure is a public interest system and that land ownership is conditional on that interest. The retained rights provide the foundations for Parliament's authority to regulate the many different aspects of the ownership and use of land in the overall public interest, while still recognising the private ownership of land as an important part of that interest.

The entrenchment of this position, with the other modernising and reforming changes proposed for the current system of land tenure, might be expected not only to create a 'new system' of land tenure in Scotland. It could foster a whole new climate around the land issue by redressing the balance of presumption in dealing with land ownership and setting the question of what might be seen as 'a taking' in a fresh context. In the final analysis, it is only this new climate, not just technical reforms, that will deliver "a final settlement on the land question in Scotland once and for all".[12]

A new system of land tenure and, with it, a new climate of opinion about land ownership, will only be built up gradually. At the end of the day, it requires a cultural change. Land ownership is a deep-seated issue in Scotland. The history of the issue will not go away. However, as part of the wider democratisation of Scotland anticipated with the new Parliament, there is need to escape the old bogey of land ownership that still shadows popular Scottish culture. Perhaps one measure of the moment when the "final settlement" has been achieved "once and for all", will be when people in Scotland can refer to *land owners* (two words) and not hear it as *landowners* (one word), with all the connotations the latter term continues to carry in Scotland. Nowhere else in Europe when you say "land owner", do people automatically think of large private estates.

Conclusions

The account of Scotland's system of land tenure in this book has been wide ranging. Too often land tenure is referred to as if it is just about, for example, landlords and tenants, superiors and vassals or conveyancing. The emphasis in this book has been on showing that land tenure is a comprehensive system encompassing the whole territory of Scotland and covering all aspects of how Scotland is owned.

This approach helps clarify that the system involves all Scotland's different natural environments – land in its fullest sense, including freshwater systems, the foreshore, coastal waters and territorial seas, the wildlife and other natural resources of these areas, as well as the ground below them and airspace above. An awareness of the system as a whole also helps show that land tenure is not just about the rural countryside, but also about all the land and buildings in Scotland's urban areas. The emphasis in the balance of land tenure issues to be addressed in urban and rural Scotland is different, but too often they are portrayed as if they are separate. There is a need for wider recognition that, for example, superiorities, land registration, succession laws, public access rights, crofting tenure, the Crown Estate and the rights of common interest shared between the owners of the flats in a tenement block, are all interconnected within the same system of land tenure.

Recognition of the full range of topics covered by the system of land tenure and of the connections between them, has to be matched by an appreciation of the boundaries of the system. The distinction needs to be recognised, particularly within the context of wider land reform, between on one hand the laws of land tenure that relate directly to property rights over land and, on the other hand, both the provisions of administrative law and other non-statutory arrangements which influence how these rights are exercised.

The land tenure system can be usefully seen as a template with which these and other factors interact. This highlights the important perspective of the overall role of the land tenure system as a technical mechanism to balance public and private interests in Scotland's land. The nature of the actual balance that the system supports, either overall or through its different elements, is determined at any point in time by society's democratic and parliamentary processes. As society's needs and values change, so the system of land tenure or aspects of it have to be modernised and reformed to match these new requirements. There is thus nothing absolute or fixed about the system of land tenure; it has to adapt or be adapted to meet contemporary circumstances.

The overall framework of the land tenure system can be seen as having two main strands. Firstly, there are the rights held in trust for the public in the name of the Crown under the authority of Parliament and in which 'the public' are, by virtue of its definition in Scots law, the people of Scotland. These rights include both the areas of the territory that remain held inalienably in trust and the rights that are retained in the other parts of the territory that are held by land owners. The rights of land ownership, including the rights that go with the leasing of land, are the second strand to the overall system of tenure. While land ownership is conditional on the public interest, the rights of land ownership also incorporate safeguards against undue encroachment by government. Both the rights held in trust for the public and the rights that go with the ownership of land can be identified, defined and categorised as part of the core structure of the land tenure system.

The description of this framework of rights in this book has included, as a prompt for further discussion, suggestions for aspects that might be modernised or reformed. The outdated nature of the current system is reflected in the number of the proposals and also gives rise to the superficially paradoxical situation where both public and private interests could be strengthened by a programme of land tenure reform.

Particular emphasis has been placed in the book on the public interest associated with the Crown because it has often been neglected and is unfamilar to many people. The public interest also occurs in a number of other guises than just the lands and rights retained in the Crown's name. These include, for example, the role of the public interest as the overall aim of the system of land tenure itself and as the authority of Parliament to further regulate the conditional nature of land ownership through administrative law. The public interest also occurs in the ownership of some lands by public bodies. However, as has been stressed, a healthy and vibrant system of private land ownership is also central to the public interest. The days have long passed when the momentum for land reform could be simplistically seen as anti-ownership, even if some particular vested landowning interests may still want to try and cast it in that light. The proposals made in this book illustrate the scope to strengthen and promote the rights of land owners generally in Scotland. Particular examples include abolishing feudal superiorities, burdens and charges and making the rights of owners to protect their legitimate interests more secure against the actions of other owners and of government. At the same time, there is the scope for reforms to strike a new and positive balance between the freedoms and responsibilities that go with land ownership. The issue for Scotland is to increase, not decrease, the number of land owners and a reformed system of land tenure is an essential base for any wider reforms to achieve that.

While some particular land tenure reforms have been suggested in this book, they are only intended as examples of possible reforms. Other suggestions will emerge as the debate progresses and, in due course, it will be up to the democratically elected representatives of the people of Scotland in the new Scottish Parliament to decide the way forward.

It is, of course, only the existence of the Parliament which will make it a realistic possibility to even have a programme of land tenure reform and some of the reasons why Members of the Scottish Parliament can be expected to take an early interest in this issue have already been outlined. One aspect of this is the responsibilities the Parliament will have for land tenure. The Parliament will, by its existence, have a procedural or technical responsibility for land tenure, in the sense that Scots property law will be part of the devolved responsibilities of the Parliament. However, by virtue of this jurisdiction, the Parliament takes on a wider responsibility – the responsibility on behalf of the people of Scotland for the overall stewardship of Scotland's land and natural resources.

The Parliament's responsibilities for land tenure will make it part of the system of land tenure. The current system, dating from the last millennium, is traditionally represented in terms of the feudal hierarchy of God, the Paramount Superior and superiors and vassals. In a reformed system, the priority of interests might be seen more appropriately in terms of the sovereignty of the people, the democracy of the Parliament, and the property rights of land owners. These three components are the core ingredients in reforming land tenure to produce a distinctive and sustainable new system for the needs of Scotland in the new millennium.

Notes

Chapter 1

1. From Wightman (1996).
2. See Callander (1987) for a comprehensive account of the way the pattern of land ownership in Scotland has evolved over the centuries.
3. For example, the Deeside and Alford District in Aberdeenshire – see Callander (1987).
4. It has been estimated, for example, that at least 25% of the estates in Scotland over 1000 acres have been held by the same families for over 400 years. For further details see Callander (1987).
5. Quoted in Callander (1987).
6. Understanding land tenure at a technical level has been helped by the publication of major new legal texts on the subject in the last ten years – see Gordon (1989) and Reid (1993). Other more introductory accounts are also now available – see, for example, McAllister & Guthrie (1992).
7. These committees were named after their Chairmen. For their reports see Reid (1963), Halliday (1966), Henry (1969).
8. This was approved as part of the Scottish Law Commission's 4th Programme of Law Reform (see Scottish Law Commission, 1990b).
9. See Scottish Law Commission (1997a).
10. See Gordon (1989).
11. See Scottish Law Commission (1997a).
12. See, for example, Dingwall-Fordyce (1996) and Nicol (1997).
13. For this observation, see Reid (1993).
14. Reid (1993).
15. See, for example, MacGregor (1993), Hunter (1995), Bryden (1996) and Wightman (1996).

Chapter 2

1. A point illustrated by William Ogilvie's writings in the 18th century, recently re-published as "Birthright in Land" (1997).
2. Lord Sewel, Minister for Agriculture, Fisheries and the Environment at the Scottish Office, in press release on 31st October 1997 announcing the publication of a new rural policy document.
3. Professor Bryan MacGregor (1993), Dr James Hunter (1995), Professor John Bryden (1996) and Professor David McCrone (1997).
4. Callander (1987).

5. Scottish Labour Party Manifesto (1997) : "An immediate study into the system of land ownership and management in Scotland as a basis for future land reform under a Scottish Parliament – for example, by examining with the Scottish Law Commission options for abolishing Scotland's outdated system of feudalism by removing the rights of feudal superiority".

6. As per the McEwen Lecturers under 3 above.

7. The Convention of Scottish Local Authorities (COSLA) has a land reform group under its Rural Affairs Committee; the Church and Nation Committee of the Church of Scotland is preparing a report on land ownership for the 1998 General Assembly; the Free Church of Scotland and the SNP's Scottish Land Commission are two other examples of bodies that produced reports on land ownership in 1997.

8. An obvious rural example is changes to the European Common Agricultural Policy.

9. This point was made by Professor McCrone in his 1997 McEwen Lecture.

10. A point made by Jim Hunter in his 1995 McEwen Lecture.

11. See, for example, McCrone (1997); also the unattributed Scottish Office quote in the Scotsman that is reproduced in Ogilvie (1997).

12. The land issue directly involves the departmental interests of several Ministers (Sewel, McLeish, Wilson, MacDonald). Sewel, Wilson and MacDonald have longstanding personal interests in the topic, as do the only other two current Scottish Office Ministers, Dewar and Galbraith.

13. Part of this is Scotland's relatively distinct form of legal system. Scotland is one of the few countries in the world that has an inter-mixed system of Roman and civil law traditions (see White & Willock, 1993).

14. See Callander (1987).

15. The possibility of these wider changes has been made significantly easier by the major new legal texts describing the existing system (Gordon, 1989, Reid, 1993).

16. For example, wardholding and boccage (in Gordon, 1989); see also Callander (1987).

17. Paisley (1988).

Chapter 3

1. See Ryan (1984).

2. Denman (1978).

3. MacCormick (1982).

4. MacGregor (1993).

5. This has tended to inhibit recognition of general principles that could

form the basis of a unified property system in Scots law – (see Reid, 1993).

6. See Gordon (1989).
7. Property law generally is concerned with 'rights in things' and these rights are known in Scots law as *real rights*. These rights of property law are contrasted with *personal rights*, which are covered by the law of obligation. Real rights include ownership, lease, security and others – (see Reid, 1993).
8. Denman (1978).
9. Overseas Development Institute (1995).
10. Reid (1993).
11. Beddard (1993).
12. For example: *Sustainable Development: the UK Approach* (HMSO, 1992).
13. See Clayton (1996).

Chapter 4

1. See MacCormick (1991).
2. For example, Mitchell (1968).
3. See Deans (1995).
4. From Mitchell (1968).
5. The main references for this and the following paragraph are Wolffe (1991) and Mitchell (1968).
6. Follows Marshall (1995).
7. See Edwards (1992) for the use of the Treaty against the introduction of the Community Charge or Poll Tax in Scotland before England.
8. See McCrone (1992).
9. The main references for this paragraph are Wolffe (1991) and Mitchell (1968).
10. The long disputed issue over the standard flown by the Queen in Scotland is a particular example of differences that can exist and illustrates the role of the Lord Lyon (Scotland's Lyon King of Arms) from time to time in defending matters relating to Scotland's national sovereignty against constitutional advice from England's Garter King of Arms (Atholl,1995).
11. See, for example, Adamson (1995).
12. For the draft Constitution, see MacCormick (1991).
13. See Barrow (1965).
14. See MacKinnon (1924) and Barrow (1965).
15. Lord Cooper quoted in Deans (1995).
16. See Barrow (1965).
17. See Adamson (1995).
18. Adamson (1995).
19. Scottish Law Commission (1991).

20. Reid (1993).
21. For these, see Atholl (1995).

Chapter 5

1. MacCormick (1991).
2. See Mitchell (1968). The current government proposes to incorporate the ECHR into UK law.
3. See Gordon (1989).
4. See Mitchell (1968).
5. McCrone (1992).
6. An example of the increase over recent years has been the greater role for the Scottish Grand Committee in legislation (state/statutes) for Scotland.
7. See Reid (1993).
8. For example, see Denman (1978).
9. See Callander (1987).
10. For example, the Macaulay Land Use Research Institute's Land Cover of Scotland.

Chapter 6

1. The main reference in this section on the European Convention on Human Rights is Beddard (1993).
2. See Erskine (1879).
3. See Rowan-Robinson (1990).
4. From Cowie (1983).
5. Rowan-Robinson and Ross (1993).
6. Rowan-Robinson and Ross (1993).
7. Soper (1983).
8. See Hofer (1992).
9. Reid (1994).
10. See Erskine (1879).
11. See Reid (1994) and Gordon (1989).
12. Rowan-Robinson and Ross (1993).
13. Soper (1983).
14. Scherer and Attig (1983).
15. See, for example, Byrne (1995).
16. See, for example, Rowan-Robinson (1993).
17. See Graham (1993).
18. Listed in unpublished paper by Lands Tribunal for Scotland, 1994.

Chapter 7

1. The draft legislation to establish the Scottish Parliament includes special provisions relating to the rivers Tweed and Esk.
2. As proposed in Reid (1993).

Chapter 8

1. For example, see the Introduction to any recent Crown Estate Commission Annual Report.
2. Section 1(5) of the Act states: "The validity of transactions entered into by the Commissioners shall not be called in question on any suggestion of their not having acted in accordance with the provisions of this Act regulating the exercise of their powers, or of their having otherwise acted in excess of their authority, nor shall any person dealing with the Commissioners be concerned to inquire as to the extent of their authority or the observance of any restrictions on the exercise of their powers."
3. Crown Estate Commission Annual Report 1997.
4. For example, the 1979 case against the Fairlie Yacht Club.
5. The Forestry Commission represents something of a parallel to the CEC. The Commissioners are appointed by the Queen, while the Secretary of State has a power of direction over its operations in Scotland.

Chapter 9

1. See Birnie (1990).
2. In Birnie (1990).
3. See Reid (1993).
4. Gordon (1989).
5. See, for example, Cleaver and Irvine (1995).
6. There might be some parallels between the reform of the CEC and the changes already made to the Forestry Commission by separating its regulatory and land management sides into the Forestry Authority and Forest Enterprise. For the CEC's ambitions to be just a landlord, see Crown Estate Commission (1996).
7. The former from the Scottish Office Fact Sheet (1995), the latter from Downie and Davis (1991) for the government's Joint National Conservation Committee.
8. Scottish Office Fact Sheet (1995).
9. From Wightman (1996).
10. See Callander (1987).
11. See Crown Estate Commission (1996).
12. Crown Estate Commission (1996).
13. See Gordon (1989).
14. See Gordon (1989).
15. See Gordon (1989).
16. See Callander (1987).
17. Barry (1990).
18. For example, see SCALPA (1996).

Chapter 10

1. See Gordon (1989).
2. Blackshaw (1996).
3. See Lindsay (1996).
4. Grant (1982).
5. Grant (1982).
6. Grant (1982).
7. Walton et al. (1995).
8. Walton et al. (1995).
9. See Bryden (1996).
10. See Callander (1987).

Chapter 11

1. For historic influence see Callander (1987). Wightman (1996) comments on their current significance.
2. See Gordon (1989).
3. See Callander (1987).
4. This 1960s estimate comes from Gordon (1989) and the more recent one from Professor Kenneth Reid (personal communication).
5. See Adamson (1995).
6. See Callander (1987).
7. See Scottish Law Commission (1990a).
8. Scottish Law Commission (1990a).
9. For example, by the Convenor of the Scottish Landowners Federation – Dingwall-Fordyce (1996).
10. For an account of European examples see, the appendix by Tony Carty in Highlands and Islands Development Board (1978).

Chapter 12

1. Reid (1993).
2. Reid (1993).
3. For the seldom told story of common land in Scotland, see Callander (1987).
4. Reid (1993).
5. See Scottish Law Commission (1990c) (1997).
6. For an example of those questioning survival, see Reid (1993); for evidence of survival see Callander (1987).
7. See Callander (1987).
8. See Callander (1987).

Chapter 13

1. See Reid (1993).
2. As in, for example, Reid (1993).
3. As suggested in Reid (1993).

4. Scottish Law Commission (1990c).
5. Gordon (1989).
6. Gordon (1989).
7. Scottish Law Commission (1991).
8. As expressed, for example, in Reid (1993).
9. Reid (1993).
10. Gordon (1989).
11. Reid (1993).
12. Reid (1993).
13. See Callander (1987).
14. For example, Gordon (1989).
15. Reid (1993).
16. Gordon (1989).
17. Scottish Law Commission (1997a).
18. Whitty (1988).
19. For example, Gordon (1989).
20. Brubaker (1995).
21. Brubaker (1995).
22. For example, see Reid (1994).

Chapter 14

1. See, for example, Denman (1978) and Reid (1993).
2. See, for example, Rankine (1909 & 1916) and McAllister (1989 & 1993).
3. For leasehold casualties, see Scottish Law Commission (1997b).
4. Scottish Law Commission (1997b).
5. See McAllister (1995).
6. See Hunter (1997).
7. See Scottish Land Commission (1996).
8. Gordon (1989).
9. Gordon (1989).
10. Gordon (1989).
11. Gordon (1989).
12. See, for example, Maitland (1996).
13. From Duncan (1992).
14. McAllister & Guthrie (1992).
15. Gordon (1989).
16. For a current example, see Millennium Forest for Scotland Trust (1996).

Chapter 16

1. See, for example, Scottish Law Commission (1991).
2. See, for example, Scottish Land Commission (1996).
3. See, for example quote in McCrone (1997).

4. See Callander (1986).
5. For example, Hunter (1995), Wightman (1996), McCrone (1997).
6. Scottish Law Commission (1991).
7. MacCormick (1997).
8. For a description of these, see Chapters 4 and 5.
9. See MacCormick (1997).
10. Scottish Office (1997).
11. Lord Sewel, Minister at the Scottish Office for Agriculture, Fisheries and the Environment, in speech quoted in Scotland on Sunday, 9th November 1997.
12. Statement by Brian Wilson, MP, Minister at the Scottish Office for Industry and Education, quoted in *Scotland on Sunday*, 2nd November 1997. The first part of his sentence reads: "There's a real momentum within the Scottish Office team behind addressing these long-standing issues and getting a final . . ."

References

Adamson, N. (1995) *The Crown and Government* in The Crown, Stair Encyclopaedia of Scots Law, Vol.7, Butterworths, Edinburgh

Agnew, C. (1995) *Royal Styles, Title and Armourial Bearings in Scotland* in The Crown, Stair Encyclopaedia of Scots Law, Vol.7, Butterworths, Edinburgh

Barrow, G. (1965), *Robert Bruce and the Community of the Realm* Edinburgh University Press

Beddard, R. (1993), *Human Rights & Europe* Grotius Publications, Cambridge

Berkes, F. (editor) (1989), *Common Property Resources: Ecology and Community Based Sustainable Development* Belhaven Press, London

Birnie, P. (1990), *Sea Fisheries* Stair Encyclopaedia of Scots Law, Butterworths, Edinburgh

Blackshaw, A. (1996), *The Basis of Public Access to Land in Scotland* Draft September 1996, SWCL, Perth

Bracewell-Milnes, B. (1982), *Land & Heritage: The Public Interest in Personal Ownership* Hobart Paper 93, Institute of Economic Affairs, London

Brubaker, E. (1995), *Property Rights in the Defense of Nature* Earthscan, London

Bryden, J.M. (1996), *Land Tenure and Rural Development in Scotland* Third McEwen Lecture on Land Tenure in Scotland, Rural Forum, Perth

Byrne, J. (1995), *Ten Arguments for the Abolition of the Regulatory Takings Doctrine* Ecology Law Quarterly

Callander, R.F. (1986), *The Law of the Land* in Land: Ownership & Use, edited Hulbert, J., Fletcher Society, Dundee

Callander, R.F. (1987), *A Pattern of Landownership in Scotland* Haughend Publications, Finzean

Clayton, A. (1996), *Sustainability* Earthscan, London

Cleator, B. & Irvine, M. (1995), A *Review of Legislation Relating to the Coast and Marine Environment in Scotland* Scottish Natural Heritage Review No.30, SNH Perth

Corbett, G. & Logie, D. (1997) *Scotland's Rural Housing: At the Heart of Communities* Shelter/Rural Forum, Perth

Cowie, G. (1983), *Background and Concept* in Compulsory Purchase in Scotland, Law Society of Scotland, Edinburgh

Crown Estate Commission (1996 & 1997), *Annual Report* London

Deans, M. (1995), *Scots Public Law* T. & T. Clark, Edinburgh

Denman, D.R. (1978), *The Place of Property: A New Recognition of the Function and Form of Property Rights in Land* Geographical Publications, Herts.

Denman, D.R. (1980), *Land in a Free Society* Centre for Policy Studies, London

Dingwall-Fordyce, A. (1996), *Scottish Landowners Federation Evidence to SNP Land Commission* Aberdeen, May 1996

Downie, A.J. & Davies, L.M. (1991), *Synopsis of survey data held by the Marine Nature Conservation Review* MNCR Occasional Report 15, JNCC, Peterborough

Duncan, A.G.M. (1992), *Scottish Legal Terms* Butterworths, Edinburgh

Edwards, D. (1992), *The Treaty of Union: More Hints of Constitutionalism* Legal Studies No.12

Erskine, J. (1879), *An Institute of the Law of Scotland* 8th Edition

Gordon, W.M. (1989), *Scottish Land Law* W. Green, Edinburgh

Graham, K.H.R. (1993), *Scottish Land Court: Practice & Procedure* Butterworths, Edinburgh

Grant, M. (1982), *Urban Planning Law* Sweet & Maxwell, London

Halliday, J. (1966) *Report on Conveyancing Legislation and Practice* Cmnd. 3118, HMSO

Henry, G. (1969) *A Scheme for Registration of Titles to Land in Scotland* Cmnd. 4137 HMSO

Highlands & Islands Development Board (1978), *Proposals for Changes in the Highlands and Islands Development (Scotland) Act 1965 to allow more effective powers over rural land use* HIDB, Inverness

HMSO (1992), *Sustainable Development: The UK Approach* London

Hofer, D. (1992), *Effectiveness of Wildlife Management Systems in USA, Great Britain, Germany and Italy* Proceedings of 4th North American Symposium on Society and Resource Management, Wisconsin

Hunter, J. (1995), *Towards a Land Reform Agenda for a Scots Parliament* Second McEwen Lecture on Land Tenure in Scotland, Rural Forum Perth

Hunter, J. (1997), *Progressing Community Ownership and Promoting New Types of Rural Settlement* Paper Presented to Highlands & Islands Convention, July 1997

Lindsay, Earl of (1996), Minister for the Environment at the Scottish Office, quoted in '*Rural Briefing: November 1996*' Bell-Ingram, Perth

MacCormick, N. (1982), *Legal Right and Social Democracy* Clarendon Press

MacCormick, N. (1991), *An Idea for a Scottish Constitution* in Edinburgh Essays in Public Law, edited Finnie, Hainsworth & Walker, Edinburgh University Press

MacCormick, N. (1995), *Sovereignty: Myth and Reality* Scottish Affairs No.11

MacCormick, N. (1997), *The English Constitution, the British State and the Scottish Anomaly* British Academy Lecture 1997, in press Scottish Affairs, University of Edinburgh

MacGregor, B. (1993), *Land Tenure in Scotland* First McEwen Lecture on Land Tenure in Scotland, Rural Forum, Perth

McAllister, A. (1989), *Scottish Law of Leases* Butterworths, Edinburgh

McAllister, A. & Guthrie, T.G. (1993), *Scottish Property Law* Butterworths, Edinburgh

McCrone, D. (1992), *Understanding Scotland: The Sociology of a Stateless Nation* Routledge, London

McCrone, D. (1997), *Land, Democracy and Culture in Scotland* Fourth McEwen Lecture on Land Tenure in Scotland, Rural Forum, Perth

MacKinnon, J.M. (1924), *The Constitutional History of Scotland* Longman Green

Maitland, P. (1996), *Review of Policies Concerning Freshwater Fisheries in Scotland* WWF Scotland, Aberfeldy

Marshall, E. (1995), *General Principles of Scots Law* W. Green, Edinburgh

Millennium Forest for Scotland Trust (1996) *Specimen Offer of Grant* MFST, Glasgow

Mitchell, J.D.B. (1968), *Constitutional Law* 2nd Edition, W. Green, Edinburgh

Murray, A. (1995) *Officers of State* in The Crown, Stair Encyclopaedia of Scots Law, Vol.7, Butterworths, Edinburgh

Nicol, R. (1997), *The Scottish Feudal System of Land Tenure – Can it be Improved* Paper to Scottish Landowners Federation Annual Conference, Battleby, April 1997

Ogilvie, W. (1997), *Birthright in Land* Othila Press, London

Overseas Development Institute (1995) *Land Reform: New Seeds on Old Ground* Natural Resource Perspectives No. 6, London

Paisley, R. (1988), Phd. Thesis, University of Aberdeen

Pryde, G.S. (1950), *The Treaty of Union of Scotland and England* Nelsons, Edinburgh

Rankine, J. (1909), *The Law of Landownership in Scotland* 4th Edition, Sweet & Maxwell, Edinburgh

Rankine, J. (1916), *A Treatise on the Law of Leases in Scotland* 3rd Edition W. Green, Edinburgh

Reid, C.T. (1994), *Nature Conservation Law* W. Green/Sweet & Maxwell, Edinburgh

Reid, C.T. (editor)(1992), *Environmental Law in Scotland* W. Green/Sweet & Maxwell, Edinburgh

Reid, K. (1993) *Property Law* Stair Encyclopaedia of Scots Law, Vol.18, Butterworths, Edinburgh

Reid, Lord (1963) *Report on Registration of Title to Land in Scotland* Cmnd. 2032 HMSO

Rowan-Robinson, J. (1990), *Compulsory Purchase and Compensation: The Law in Scotland* W. Green, Edinburgh

Rowan-Robinson, J. & Ross, A. (1993), *Compensation for Environmental Protection in Britain: A Legislative Lottery* Journal of Environmental Law Vol. 5, No. 2

Ryan, A. (1984), *Property and Political Theory* Blackwell, Oxford

SCALPA (1996) *Scottish Campaign for Public Angling Newsletters* Edinburgh

Scherer, D. & Attig, T. (editors)(1983) *Ethics and the Environment* Prentice-Hall, New Jersey

Scottish Land Commission (1996), *Public Policy Towards Land in Scotland* Consultative Report, Volume 1, Commissioners' Report, SNP, London

Scottish Law Commission (1990a), *Succession* Report 124, SLC, Edinburgh

Scottish Law Commission (1990b), *Fourth Programme of Law Reform* Report 126, SLC, Edinburgh

Scottish Law Commission (1990c), *Law of Tenement* Discussion Paper 91, SLC, Edinburgh

Scottish Law Commission (1991), *Property Law: Abolition of the Feudal System* Discussion Paper 93, SLC, Edinburgh

Scottish Law Commission (1993), *Annual Report* HMSO, Edinburgh

Scottish Law Commission (1994), *Annual Report* HMSO, Edinburgh

Scottish Law Commission (1997a), *Fifth Programme of Law Reform* Report, SLC, Edinburgh

Scottish Law Commission (1997b), *Discussion Paper on Leasehold Casualties* Discussion Paper 102, SLC, Edinburgh

Scottish Office (1997) Scotland's Parliament White Paper, Cmnd. 3658, Stationery Office

Soper, P. (1983), *Taking Issues* in Scherer, D. & Attig, T. (editors) *Ethics and the Environment* Prentice-Hall, New Jersey

Walton, W., Ross-Robertson, A., Rowan-Robinson, J.(1995), *The Precautionary Principle and the UK Planning System* Environmental Law and Management Vol. 7 Issue 1.

White, R. & Willock, I. (1993), *The Scottish Legal System* Butterworths, Edinburgh

Wightman, A. (1996), *Who Owns Scotland* Canongate, Edinburgh

Wolffe, W.J. (1991), *Crown and Prerogative in Scots Law* in Edinburgh Essays in Public Law, edited Finnie, Hainsworth & Walker, Edinburgh University Press

Index

About the Author

Robin Callander's previous book, *A Pattern of Landownership in Scotland*, published in 1987, has been widely recognised as a major contribution to the land debate. He has also been responsible for initiating and guiding the influential annual McEwen Lectures on Land Tenure in Scotland. He has over twenty years experience as a self-employed adviser on rural land use and community development issues in Scotland. He owns and manages 500 hectares of land with three partners near to his home on Deeside where he lives with his wife and three daughters. He can also claim to have been one of Scotland's foremost drystane dykers and the first ever drystane dyker by Royal Appointment to the Queen.

Also published by Canongate Books

WHO OWNS SCOTLAND
Andy Wightman

Drawing on a wide range of sources, *Who Owns Scotland* not only provides the most comprehensive listings of who actually owns Scotland but also analyses the current pattern of landownership and how it has evolved over the centuries. The book reviews the history and politics of land reform in Scotland, examines the extent of available information on this controversial subject, and provides a critique of the existing ownership pattern and land tenure system. *Who Owns Scotland* is essential reading for anyone who cares about the future of this country, both its land and people.

'*This is a most remarkable and very timely book. It is remarkable in the thoroughness of its research, the scope of its recommendations and the breadth of its vision. It is timely in that its appearance coincides with a growing conviction, right across Scotland, that action both can and must be taken to reform the means by which our country regulates and controls the ownership of land.*'

James Hunter

'*For anyone with some knowledge of or curiosity about Britain's property-owning classes, [this] book is required reading.*'

Financial Times

'*[Wightman's] cool, calm study is an indictment of the current position, and his solutions to overcome the most concentrated and secretive pattern of land ownership in Europe are . . . radical and controversial.*'

The Herald

ISBN 0 86241 585 3   **£14.99**